I.

MW01596439

In accordance with c. 827,
permission to publish is granted on
March 17, 2014, by
Most Reverend Francis J. Kane,
Vicar General of the Archdiocese of
Chicago

Permission to publish is an official
declaration of ecclesiastical
authority that the material is free
from doctrinal and moral error.

No legal responsibility is assumed
by the grant of this permission.

DEDICATION

I dedicate this book to Jesus, through the Blessed
Virgin Mary, for the Glory of God (Totus Tuus).

SPIRITUAL THANKSGIVING

Saint John Paul II - Ann Patterson
Father Francis Budovic - Dr. Dean Murphy
Bishop Roger Kaffer - Fr. Piotr Gnoinsk
Fr. Peter Mary Rookey - Joseph Reinholtz

THANKSGIVING

A special thanks to the following
for helping with this book:

Charmaine Murphy
Monica Hammerschmidt
Eileen Craig - Celeste Donner
Solita De LaPaz - Garrett Fosco
Elizabeth Pukala – Charmaine Simikoski

Bible Citation
Douay-Rheims, 2007 printing, Copyright ©2002.
Loreto Publications. All rights reserved.

The New Catholic Answer Bible, 2005, Our
Sunday Visitor, Inc. Copyright ©1970, by
Catholic Bible Publishers. Wichita, Kansas 67201.

TABLE OF CONTENTS

INTRODUCTION: Angels of the New Era
I. BIBLICAL ANGELIC INSIGHTS:

I. Introduction: Angels of the New Era
Teach Your Soul How to Fly in Thirty-three Days!

A young man named Ben was walking with his Angel during a pilgrimage to the Holy Land. The Angel was tall and had very large wings. Ben was a feisty but cynical guy who liked to challenge the status quo. As they approached Bethlehem, Ben said to his Angel, "There are so many problems in the world today such as drugs, violence, divorce, wars, stealing, abortion, corruption in politics, and look, even here in Bethlehem! Look at that monster twenty-eight-foot high prison wall that they are building. Where are the principles of freedom? What a disaster!"

There was a slight pause, and then Ben complained, "Jesus Christ was born two thousand years ago and there are still so many problems in the world. I guess it didn't do any good, did it?"

The Angel's piercing eyes looked at him but kept on walking. After a short time, they came upon three children playing in the mud. The Angel said with his thunderous voice, "Look, Ben, at these children. Soap was invented four thousand years ago and they are still dirty. I guess the soap did not do any good, did it?" There was a long pause then, being a tough nut to crack, Ben argued, "This is different. These children should have listened to their mothers and stayed out of the mud. Even now, there is nothing wrong with the soap, you just have to apply it."

The Angel said, "It is the same thing for the world today. God sent our Heavenly Mother to ask us not to go into the spiritual mud, but we don't listen. Even today, all the graces to bring peace and joy to Earth are available through Jesus Christ's church. All we have to do is apply it." Ben was in awe and then said, "Grace?"

"Yes, grace! The truth is, without the grace of God through Jesus Christ, you humans would have blown yourselves up a long time ago," replied the Angel.

"Go on," invited Ben.

The Angel continued, "Mental prayer (meditation) is the key to applying the grace of Jesus Christ and His Church effectively into your lives and into the world."

"What is mental prayer (meditation)?" Ben asked.

"Ben, God created you with a body and a soul. Mental prayer is to use the three powers of your soul, the Memory, the Intellect, and the Will to encounter God."

"Encounter God?" Ben asked. "At times, God feels so far away."

"With mental prayer, the Kingdom of God is at hand! Yes, God is speaking to you all the time.

Mental prayer will help you experience God speaking to you." "I thought God only spoke to Moses through the Burning Bush," stated Ben.

"Follow me," said the Angel. Ben followed the Angel past the check point of the large wall around the town of Bethlehem and into the Church. The Angel pointed out the star located underneath the altar where Jesus was born.

"Here is where it happened! Jesus Christ is God's Word made flesh and He spoke to men. God continues to speak through the Gospel and the Holy Spirit. The normal gifts of the Holy Spirit include wisdom, knowledge, and understanding. These gifts come as thoughts to the mind, especially during mental prayer!" the Angel explained.

"How come God feels so far away?" asked Ben.

"Because there are other voices that speak to you that are not from Heaven. These are temptations, distractions, and confusions. If you have faith, love, and are committed to the truth, you will hear God's voice!" exclaimed the Angel.

"How do I know when God is speaking?" asked Ben. "You will know the voice is from Heaven because the gifts of the Holy Spirit will always encourage you on the path that gets closer to God. Jesus's Church describes that path.

"Anything else?" asked Ben.

"God's voice also gives you the gifts of peace and joy. Peace is a gift that only comes from God and you cannot have joy without peace. Mental prayer is a spiritual exercise that can help you hear God more clearly."

"Spiritual exercises?" asked Ben.

"Spiritual exercises help develop the soul's ability to fly, so to speak. We, Angels, do this all the time. We fly to God and experience that peace and joy." Ben protested. "That sounds nice, but I attended a weekend retreat that taught St. Ignatius spiritual exercises and the whole thing went over my head. I just drew a blank. I don't think this is for me."

The Angel asked Ben, "Do you remember last year when your brother started to drive?"

"Yes," Ben chuckled. "He froze the first time he got behind the wheel. He did not know where to start. He could not decide whether to press on the gas or put it into gear or press on the brake. He gripped the steering wheel so tight that sweat came from his forehead."

The Angel said, "That is how you acted on that retreat. How was your brother after the month of driver's education?"

"He is a natural. He says he can't be without his car. It is part of his lifestyle." Ben replied.

The Angel said, "Meditation is like driving a car. Once you learn how to do it, it is easy and even fun. After a short time you will not know what to do without it. The Angels of the New Era method is teaching your soul how to fly in 33 days. One day for each year that Jesus Christ was on Earth."

"Oh yeah!" said Ben, "What is this Angel Method and where do I start?"

"You start by learning the Angel Members' prayer and repeating it often to get the grace from the good God to meditate. God is everywhere. First, you must take a moment to recall that you are with the Angels in the presence of God and pray: 'Dear God, I beg You to please give me the grace, to SPEAK to the three powers of my soul, so my memory, my intellect, and my will, will be for the greater Glory of God.'"

"Keep praying this Angel Prayer and then someday the Holy Spirit will put a burning desire in your heart to read the first Angel story in the Angels of the New Era constitution."

"Angel stories?" Ben asked.

"Yes," said the Angel. "The Constitution is based on 15 stories of Angels in the Bible that are split up into a 33 day period. As you read the story, you watch the Angel, listen to the Angel, and imitate the Angel. Each day, you read a story in the morning and you try to recall it several times during the day. As that is done, you will pick up the principles of mental prayer and your soul's wings will develop muscles to fly. Here is a copy of the Constitution."

"Does this have any use in today's society?" "Yes, it is used very effectively in advertising. Why do cola companies spend over one million dollars for a one-minute commercial when they do not even say 'buy this cola'?" asked the Angel.

"Why?" asked Ben.

"Because in one minute, they fill your memory and give your intellect something to think about. The next time that you are thirsty, your will, will prompt you to reach for their cola," said the Angel. "In addition to this, the people in the mass media use this power to move most of the world to go wherever they want. They especially move the people who do not know how to meditate."

"OK, I would like to start. As you walk with me on this pilgrimage, can you do me the favor and walk me through a sample meditation?" asked Ben.

"Yes," the Angel said, "If you say the Angel prayer several times today, tomorrow we will begin our 33-day journey. You can always conclude your encounter with God by saying, 'Dear God, we **thank you** for giving us the grace that the three powers of our soul, the memory, the intellect and the will, will always be for the greater glory of God. Amen."

I. BIBLICAL ANGELIC INSIGHTS:

Teach Your Soul How to Fly in Thirty-three Days!

Day 1 The subject is "The Preciousness of Life on Earth!"

"Are you ready, Ben, to learn how to meditate?" "Only, if you help me," Ben replied. "I need wisdom." "Do you know that the first step in wisdom is to know the shortness of life?" (see Psalm 90 for the full quotation). "Can we take that first step?" asked Ben. "OK. Take off your shoes. Today, we will walk through the meditation together as we walk along this sandy beach. We will scoop up a handful of sand." The subject for meditation is the destiny of our eternal souls.

Picture a beautiful, large, sandy beach along the ocean and take a moment to recall that you are with the Angels in the presence of God. Pray: "Dear God, I beg You to please give me the grace that the three powers of my soul—my memory, my intellect, and my will—will be for the greater glory of God." Also ask God for a specific grace: "Help me to appreciate the gift of being alive."

The Memory: In which we recall the subject and ask questions such as WHAT—What do I see? What do I hear? What do I feel? What do I smell?

Ben smiles and says, "It is a beautiful sunny day, and I see a very long, sandy beach. I feel the soft sand underfoot as we go for a walk. The sun is warm; the gentle breeze is cool and refreshing. The white seagulls are swooping down for food and making a high-sounding chirp. The white clouds look like a soft cotton ball floating in the blue sky. The waves can be heard crashing on the shore." "Now scoop up a handful of sand as we continue to walk," said the Angel. "What do you notice?" "While looking closer at the many grains in my hand, I notice that most are light brown, some are black, and others are white. The grains are numerous; however, the amount of sand is so very small compared to what is on the beach and underwater," said Ben.

The Intellect: In which we reflect and analyze the subject. We often ask the questions why and how.

"Ben, how many days are there in a year?" "Three hundred sixty-five," Ben answered. "How many days are there in 100 years?" "That would be 100 times 365 or 36,500 days," Ben answered again. "There are at least 36,500 grains of sand in your hand. If you live to be 100 years old, each grain would represent a day in your life on Earth. During your life, some days are exceptionally good, as can be seen in the white specs. Some days are tough, as can be seen in the black specs. Most days are average, as can be seen in the light brown specs.

Even though the grains are numerous, they are soon gone when we let them trickle out of our hands. Every day that passes by on Earth is like a grain of sand trickling through our hands. Every day, there are less remaining."

"If the small amount of sand in your hand represents your life on Earth, the large amount of sand on the beach and under the water represents your life after Earth. The way you spend the days of life on Earth determines how you will spend all the days of life after Earth. Jesus Christ gives us many opportunities on Earth to build up our treasure in Heaven" (see Matthew 6:20).

"There are three paths one can take: the first path consists of endeavoring to love God with all our hearts, minds, souls, and bodies, and our neighbors as ourselves. During our eternal life in Heaven, each day will be filled with joy so great, it is unimaginable. 'For eye has not seen, nor ear heard, neither has it entered into the heart of man, what things God has prepared for those who love Him.' (1 Corinthians 2:9). We will shine like the bright stars in the sky."

"Forever is such a long time," interrupted Ben, "won't we get bored?" "Will you get bored with power or beauty or truth or knowledge or peace or love or goodness?" Actually, when you experience how awesome God IS, you will be saying in your soul for all eternity, "WWWWWooooowwwww!"

"The second path consists of doing the minimal to get by and of keeping our soul out of the state of mortal sin. During our life after Earth, we will spend a long time suffering in the fires of purgatory (see Matthew 5:26, 1 Cor. 3:15). After this, we will experience incredible, unimaginable joy in Heaven, but not as much joy as the first path. We will shine like the very dim stars in the sky."

"On the third path, we let our souls fall into the state of mortal sin, blame and curse God for our foolishness and then die without repenting. During our eternally long life after Earth in Hell, each day will be filled with tortures so terrible and painful that they cannot be imagined. The truth, that we are in Hell through our own fault, tortures us even more." Actually, Hell is so horrible, you will be saying in your soul for all eternity, "Ooooowwwww!"

"Think about how much sand there is out there compared to the small amount in our hands and realize that eternity is even longer than the days/number of grains of sand on the beach. Know for sure that the days in eternity are greater than all the grains of sand on the entire planet Earth. This thought helps us realize that the short time we are given here on Earth is very precious and important.

Your life on Earth may even be less than a hundred years or an even smaller handful of sand. God let us know that we can build up our treasure while on Earth (see Matthew 6:20). When we get to Heaven, we cannot build up our treasure, we can only enjoy it. We must ask ourselves; how do we take advantage of the precious time we have on Earth?"

We make a resolution . . . The Will: "Ben, what resolution are you going to make regarding this subject?"

"I will try to do my best to choose the first path every day during our short life on Earth. I promise to get to know and love Jesus, by learning to pray the Rosary mysteries and reading the Bible. I promise to be true to my covenant with God and to be united to Jesus by receiving Him in Holy Communion. To build up my treasure in Heaven, I will use mental prayer. I promise to beg God for the grace that the three powers of my soul—my memory, my intellect, and my will—will be for the greater glory of God," replied Ben.

"I will ask the Holy Spirit to remind me that every time I see *sand***,** I will remember how short and precious this life is, and how eternally long the afterlife will be. I will have confidence that Jesus Christ won the big W for me so my eternal 'Ooooowwwww!' will be an eternal

'WWWWWooooowwwww!'" "Very good, Ben, I can see progress in your soul already."

"The next step for this and all Angel stories is to *stop* and be quiet for five minutes, and think about the story. Pick one or two words for each—the memory, intellect, and will—and write it down. It will help you fly up to God. For three times each day, look at what you wrote down, and picture the Angel in your mind, the lessons will sink in, and God will touch you with His peace. You can come up with your own words from the meditation, but I will help you with a possible suggestion for each story."

"Why three times in a day and for how long?" asked Ben. "Because to meditate is a spiritual exercise, and not just gaining information. God speaks to you through the meditation," answered the Angel. "Think about it for a few minutes and if you find peace and joy, then stay with it longer."

What are the three words for today?

For the memory, (What do I see, hear, smell, etc.) we can use numerous sand.

For the intellect (analyze, ask why and how) we can use numerous days.

For the will (I will try to improve this in my life) we can use heavenly treasure.

"OK," said Ben. "I am writing these words down and keeping them in my pocket and I will read it on my lunch break and then before dinner and then before I go to sleep tonight."

"Excellent," said the Angel. "You may even want to do it again the first thing when you wake up." "OK, I will. I like this meditation. I think I can do it. It is not so hard," said Ben.

"Great, you will do Day 2 tomorrow on your own. If you need help just call on me, I am always at your side."

"Thanks," said Ben. "I want to fly like you do at the end of the 33 days."

Let us always close the five minutes by saying, *Dear God, I thank You for giving me the grace to Speak to the three powers of my soul, so my memory, my intellect, and my will—will always be for the greater glory of God. Amen.*

Day 2 **SUPPLEMENT:**

Before I start Day 2, I have another question.

"I will read Day 2 today, but first, can you review for me how the Angel method will teach my soul how to fly?" asked Ben.

Start out by learning the Angel prayer, *"Dear God, I beg You to please give me the grace, to speak to the three powers of my soul, so my memory, my intellect, and my will, will be for the greater Glory of God."*

Memorize it then say it every day. The Holy Spirit will put a burning desire in your heart when it is time to do the first Angel story. If you skip a day, just continue one day later.

When you are ready, read the Angel story in the morning. This is not only about knowledge, but about the powers of your soul, the memory, the intellect, and the will. It is a spiritual exercise of the soul that will help you fly. After reading it, take five minutes and use your memory to think about the Angel story. Write down a word for each of the three powers of the soul.

Throughout the day, look at the words that you wrote down, and try to remember parts of the story. In the evening, review the story one more time, and see how much you remembered. After a few days, you will see that your soul will start to develop wings.

Advice: If you feel something is chaining your soul to the ground, look at the crucifix when you beg God for the grace that the three powers of your soul, your memory, your intellect, and your will, will be for the greater glory of God.

"I could probably read this in 3 days!" Ben said. "Does this have to take 33 days?"

"Would you get into a plane with a pilot who only read information about flying a plane, or do you want a pilot who has experienced flying in a school?" replied the Angel.

"I get it. This is a school to teach the soul how to fly. This takes skill, not only information," Ben replied. "I am going to take the 33-day angel school challenge."

Day 2 1.1 ANGELS OF CHRISTMAS
Jesus's Birthday (Luke 2:1–16)

Let us take a moment to recall that we are with the Angels in the presence of God and pray: "Dear God, I beg You to please give me the grace, to SPEAK to the three powers of my soul, so my memory, my intellect, and my will, will be for the greater Glory of God."

MEMORY: What do I see? What do I hear? What do I feel? What do I smell?

We are with the shepherds in the fields. We see the bright stars twinkling on a clear night. We feel the cold air; we hear the crickets and the sheep bleating in the distance. We smell burnt wood from the fire that was made to keep us warm. We look up. We see light in the sky that gets very bright. The light takes the form of a beautiful Angel. The Angel has a soft glow around his white wings. We become afraid of the unusual but magnificent sight. His voice was young but powerful as if it echoed all the way back up to heaven.

We recall the **Angel of the Lord** appeared to the shepherds and said, "Be not afraid, I bring you tidings of great joy [good news] which shall be shared to all the people; for today in the town of David, a Savior is born to you who is Christ the Lord" (Luke 2:10–11). We look at the face of a shepherd. What do we see? The words of the Angel echo in our memory, "Be not afraid! Be not afraid! Be not afraid!"

INTELLECT: Why is the Angel saying to the shepherds "Be not afraid"? How can we imitate the Angel? God is calling the shepherds to boldly seek out the Savior and then to share the good news. God knows that fear will paralyze the shepherds.

1.1 WILL: Our resolution. First of all, we learn from the Angel to "Be not afraid." Be not afraid to get closer to our God, Jesus Christ. Especially, be not afraid to meditate. It is easy and with time, you will become a master of mental prayer. Also, be not afraid to read the Bible. No one understands everything in the Bible, so focus on what you do understand and in time God will reveal more to you. Read especially Matthew, Mark, Luke, and John. God is good. He gives us the Bible so we can know Him better. Much spiritual strength will be obtained through reading the Bible. Like the Angel, we will tell others to "Be not afraid" to get closer to God through mental prayer.

STOP: Take a five minute flight with the Angel by putting yourself in his place. Make a picture in your mind, and look at the faces.

Use the three powers of your soul: your Memory to ask, **"What do I see? What do I hear? What do I feel? What do I smell?"** Use your Intellect to analyze, **"Why and how?"** and then your Will to make a resolution in your life all for the greater glory of God. "OK, Ben, for this and all Angel stories, pick one or two words for each—the memory, intellect and will and write it down. It will help you fly up to God. For 3 times each day, look at what you wrote down and picture the Angel in your mind; the lessons will sink in and God will touch you with His peace. I suggest 12:00 noon, 6:00 p.m. and just before you go to bed at night. You may come up with your own words from the meditation, but I will help you with a possible suggestion for each story."

CLOSE THE FIVE MINUTES BY SAYING . . .
Dear God, I thank You for giving me the grace to SPEAK to the three powers of my soul, so my memory, my intellect, and my will—will always be for the greater glory of God. Amen.

The suggested word for today:
Try noon, 6:00 p.m., and nighttime.

(Memory)   "Be not afraid"
(Intellect)   "Closer to God"
(Will)   "Meditate"

Day 3 1.2 ANGELS OF CHRISTMAS
Jesus's Birthday (Luke 2:1–16)

Let us take a moment to recall that we are with the
Angels in the presence of God and pray: "Dear God,
I beg You to please give me the grace, to SPEAK to the
three powers of my soul, so my memory, my intellect,
and my will, will be for the greater Glory of God."

MEMORY: What do I see? What do I hear? What do I feel? What do I smell?

We are with the shepherds in the fields. We see the bright stars twinkling on a clear night. We feel the cold air; we hear the crickets and the sheep bleating in the distance. We smell burnt wood from the fire that was made to keep us warm. We look up. We see light in the sky that gets very bright. The light takes the form of a beautiful Angel. The Angel has a soft glow around his white wings. We become afraid of the unusual but magnificent sight. His voice was young but powerful as if it echoed all the way back up to heaven.

We recall the **Angel of the Lord** appeared to the shepherds and said, "Be not afraid, I bring you tidings of great joy (good news) which shall be shared to all the people; for today in the town of David, a Savior is born to you who is Christ the Lord" (Luke 2:10-11). We look at the face of the Angel, what do we see? The words of the Angel echo in our memory, "I bring you tidings of great joy . . . (Good News) which shall be shared for all people." "I bring you tidings of great joy . . . (Good News) which shall be shared for all people."

INTELLECT: Why is the Angel saying, "I bring you tidings of great joy (Good News)?" How can we imitate the Angel? Like the Angels of the Bible, the Angels of the New Era will also be bearers of Good News. Sometimes people see the problems of today and become complainers of bad news. We know that all these problems are the fruit of our sins. However, the Angel told Joseph to "call His name Jesus (which means God saves) for He will save them from their sins" (Matthew 1:21). So this is Good News. Jesus will save us.

1.2 WILL: We make resolutions. Angel members will have great confidence in Jesus's saving power and with great joy, remain messengers of Good News.

STOP: Take a five minute flight with the Angel by putting yourself in his place. Make a picture in your mind, and look at the faces.

Use the three powers of your soul: your Memory to ask, **"What do I see? What do I hear? What do I feel? What do I smell?"** Use your Intellect to analyze, **"Why and how?"** and then your Will to make a resolution in your life all for the greater glory of God.

CLOSE THE FIVE MINUTES BY SAYING . . .

Dear God, I thank You for giving me the grace to SPEAK to the three powers of my soul, so my memory, my intellect, and my will—will always be for the greater glory of God. Amen.

(Memory) "Tidings joy"

(Intellect) "Jesus is remedy"

(Will)   "Apply Jesus's grace"

Try to think of this story and the phrases at:

Noon, 6:00 p.m., and nighttime.

Day 4 6.1–6.2 ANGEL GABRIEL'S ANNUNCIATION To Mary: (Luke 1:26–38)

Let us take a moment to recall that we are with the Angels in the presence of God and pray: "Dear God, I beg You to please give me the grace, to SPEAK to the three powers of my soul, so my memory, my intellect, and my will, will be for the greater Glory of God."

MEMORY: What do I see? What do I hear? What do I feel? What do I smell?

MEMORY: We see the three persons in God, the Father, the Son, and the Holy Spirit looking over poor humanity on Earth that is engaged in violence and bad language. However, God smiles at what He sees in a small, humble house. It is Mary. She is about fifteen years old. She has black hair, blue eyes, and rosy cheeks. She smiles as She sews a blanket. Although She is working on Earth, Her heart is thinking of God in Heaven. God then says, "It is time," and dispatches an Angel. We see Angel Gabriel. He is dressed in white. He has large wings. There is a glow of white that surrounds him. We think of purity.

The Angel **Gabriel** was sent by God to a city of Galilee called Nazareth to a Virgin espoused to a man named Joseph, of the house of David, and the Virgin's name was Mary. And the **Angel** came in and said to Her, "Hail, full of grace, the Lord is with thee, blessed art thou among women" (Lk 1:26–28).

We see the face of the Angel as he says the first Hail Mary.

INTELLECT: The Angel Gabriel, was sent by God, is the first one to say the Hail Mary. How can we imitate the Angel?

6.1 WILL: When Angel members pray the Rosary, we will imitate the way the Angel first spoke the Hail Mary, slow and with the heart, because he was full of love and did not want to frighten Her. This type of prayer with the heart will take approximately twenty-three to twenty-four seconds for each Hail Mary. Just as it pleased God when the Angel Gabriel prayed it, it also pleases God when Angel members pray it every day.

MEMORY: We hear the Angel say, "Hail Mary, full of grace . . ." Saint Dominic called the Hail Mary, The Angelic Salutation. Once Our Lady appeared to Saint Dominic and said, "My son, do not be surprised if your sermons fail to bear the results you had hoped for. You are trying to cultivate a piece of ground which has not had any rain. Now when the Almighty God planned to renew the face of the earth, He started by sending down rain from Heaven—and this was the Angelic Salutation. In this way, God made over the world. So when you give a sermon, urge people to say my Rosary, and in this way your words will bear much fruit for souls" (<u>Secret of the Rosary, the third Rose,</u> by Saint Louis DeMontfort).

INTELLECT: How is God using the Angel? God used the Angel as a mediator between God and man to serve the One Mediator, Jesus Christ. God also can send the Blessed Virgin Mary, the Queen of the Angels, to serve Jesus Christ. God can ask us to help too.

6.2 WILL: Therefore, Angel members will be messenger servants of God to men and act in this way as mediators to serve the One Mediator, Jesus Christ (see St. Paul's letter).

STOP: Take a five minute flight with the Angel You know what to do.

(Memory)	"Hail Mary"
(Intellect)	"God sent"
(Will)	"Loving prayer"

Day 5 6.3–6.5 ANGEL GABRIEL'S ANNUNCIATION To Mary: (Luke 1:26–38)

Let us take a moment to recall that we are with the Angels in the presence of God and pray: "Dear God, I beg You to please give me the grace, to SPEAK to the three powers of my soul, so my memory, my intellect, and my will, will be for the greater Glory of God."

MEMORY: We see the three persons in God, the Father, the Son, and the Holy Spirit looking over poor humanity on Earth engaged in violence and bad language. However, God smiles at what He sees in a small, humble house. It is Mary. She is about fifteen years old. She has black hair, blue eyes, and rosy cheeks. She smiles, as She sews a blanket. Although She is working on Earth, Her heart is thinking of God in Heaven. God then says, "It is time," and dispatches an Angel. We see Angel Gabriel. He is dressed in white. He has large wings. There is a glow of white that surrounds him. We think of purity.

The Angel **Gabriel** was sent by God to a city of Galilee called Nazareth to a Virgin espoused to a man named Joseph, of the house of David, and the Virgin's name was Mary. And the **Angel** came in and said to Her, "Hail, full of grace, the Lord is with thee, blessed art thou among women" (Luke 1:26–28). The words echo over and over in our hearts as we see the beautiful Angel say, "Hail, Full of Grace . . ."

INTELLECT: Why did the Angel call Her Full of Grace?

What is Grace? Grace is God's gift or help to us. Obtaining and embracing God's grace is the key to Christianity. By watching Mary, we can learn about what grace is and how to obtain it. We spend time watching Mary as we meditate upon the mysteries of the Rosary.

6.3 WILL: Angel members will zealously pray the Rosary to obtain God's grace for their souls and for others.

MEMORY: We hear the Angel say, "Hail, full of grace" (Luke 1:28).

INTELLECT: Mary is full of grace before Jesus is living inside of Her. In order to be full of grace, Her soul had no stain of sin. Therefore, God put enmities (total separation) between Mary and the Devil, and between Her children and his children. Someday, She will crush his head, while he lies in wait of Her heel (see Genesis 3:15).

The Holy Spirit revealed to God's Church that God created Mary without original sin. You can save a baby bird that falls into the water before it drowns. You can also save it before it falls into the water. God saved Our Lady before She sinned. This is also known as the Immaculate Conception. This means that God put total separation between Mary and the

Devil (see Genesis 3:15). Therefore, Mary is rightfully called by the Angel full of grace.

6.4 WILL: Angel members will strive to imitate Mary and be full of grace, for that is very pleasing to God. Therefore we will keep a separation from us and the Devil or sin.

MEMORY: We hear the Angel say "Hail, Full of Grace

. . ." In Rue du Bac, Paris on Saturday, November 27, in the year 1830, God sent Our Lady to a novice called Saint Catherine Laboure. Heaven asked that she make a medal of the vision in which She, Mary, is crushing the head of the serpent. Our Lady called it the medal of the Immaculate Conception. God confirmed the importance of the vision on the medal by causing so many miracles to happen through the medal that people changed its name to the Miraculous Medal. God has ways of letting us know how to highlight certain Biblical passages. God also preserved Saint Catherine's body. One hundred twenty-five years after her death, her body is incorrupt and can be seen in a glass coffin. She is the only incorrupt saint who has her eyes open. This is truly a spectacular miracle.

INTELLECT: Why does God make such spectacular miracles regarding the Immaculate Conception? In spiritual battles, God does not want anyone to be confused about which side they should be on.

6.5 WILL: Angel members will always be among the Woman's children and not the Devil's children. God will shower many graces on Angel members who have the Miraculous Medal.

STOP: Take a five-minute flight with the Angel by putting yourself in his place. Make a picture in your mind, and look at the faces.

Use the three powers of your soul: your Memory to ask, **"What do I see? What do I hear? What do I feel? What do I smell?"** Use your Intellect to analyze, **"Why and how?"** and then your Will to make a resolution in your life all for the greater glory of God.

CLOSE THE FIVE MINUTES BY SAYING . . .
Dear God, I thank You for giving me the grace to SPEAK to the three powers of my soul, so my memory, my intellect, and my will—will always be for the greater glory of God. Amen.

(Memory)	"Full of Grace"
(Intellect)	"Saving a Bird"
(Will)	"Embrace the Grace"

Day 6 2.1–2.2 GOOD ANGELS BATTLE
The Bad Angels: (Revelation 12)

Let us take a moment to recall that we are with the Angels in the presence of God and pray: "Dear God, I beg You to please give me the grace, to SPEAK to the three powers of my soul, so my memory, my intellect, and my will, will be for the greater Glory of God."

MEMORY: We are in Heaven and everything is beautiful! We see the glory of God. We see billions of Angels. We hear the singing, and we feel God's peace and His love. We see the Angels. They are all happy. They shine with different degrees of beauty and brightness. We see the most beautiful and bright Angel named Lucifer. God has given him much treasure in Heaven. Lucifer shines with a high degree of glory in Heaven. God instructs the Angels to help the humans during their pilgrimage on Earth: To live the law of love, build up much treasure in Heaven, and then return home to God. There is a pause. We see Lucifer's face turn envious at the human's treasures in heaven, for it could exceed his own (see Wisdom 2:24). We see the expression of his face turn very angry. We hear him say, "I will not serve!" We see a huge Angel named Michael. He is about eight feet tall and has large wings. We hear St. Michael say, "Who is like unto God?" St. Michael grabs him like a spear and thrusts him out of Heaven like lightning towards the earth. Several of his minions go with him. God says to the Angels: "Do not interfere with the human's free will, but out of love, help them journey well and to come back home. All the graces from Jesus Christ's sacrifice are available to them. Do your best to get them to embrace the grace. If they resist and choose to persevere in following Satan to Hell, so be it." **Michael** and **his Angels** fought with the dragon who is the devil and Satan (see Revelation 12:7–9).

Behold, a great sign appeared in the sky, a Woman clothed with the sun, the moon under Her feet and on Her head a crown of twelve stars (Revelation 12:1–2).

The (devil) was angry with the Woman, and went to make war with the rest of Her (children) who keep the commandments of God and have the testimony of Jesus Christ (see Revelation 12:17). We look at the expression on the Devil's face. The anger of the Devil against the Woman and Her children echoes in our memory. "The Devil is angry with the Woman. The Devil is angry with the Woman."

INTELLECT: In the Book of Revelation, a battle is described between the Devil and his demons against Saint Michael the Archangel along with Our Lady and Her children. Saint Michael, Our Lady, and Her children always help people to know, love, and serve Jesus Christ. The Devil and his demons always tempt people to hate and rebel against Jesus Christ. How do we imitate the good Angels? The good Angels chose to serve the good God.

2.1 WILL: Angel members will serve. They will take the spiritual battle seriously; and stay on the same side as Saint Michael, Our Lady and Her children and help people to know, love and serve Jesus Christ. We will listen closely to Our Lady the Queen of the Angels. We will read and reread the messages that God sent Our Lady to deliver to us.

MEMORY: We see a huge Angel named Michael. He has a sword that gives off a bright light. We see the battle of the Angels. We look at St. Michael's face as he thrusts Lucifer out of Heaven. "The great dragon was cast out; that old serpent, who is called the Devil and Satan, who seduces the whole world, and he is cast unto the earth, and his Angels were thrown down with him . . . The accuser of our brothers is cast out" (Revelation 12: 9–10).

INTELLECT: How do we help out in this battle? How do we protect ourselves? Ask St. Michael's help and imitate his defense of the Woman and Her children.

2.2 WILL: Angel members will learn the Saint Michael Prayer and call on him often for protection, comfort, and direction. "Saint Michael the Archangel, defend us in battle. Be our safeguard against the wickedness and snares of the Devil. May God rebuke him, we humbly pray, and do thou, Oh prince of the Heavenly Host, by the Divine power of God, bind into hell, Satan and all the evil spirits who wander throughout the world seeking the ruin of souls. Amen."

STOP: Take a five minute flight with the Angel by putting yourself in his place. Make a picture in your mind, and look at the faces.

CLOSE THE FIVE MINUTES BY SAYING . . .
Dear God, I thank You for giving me the grace to SPEAK to the three powers of my soul, so my memory, my intellect, and my will—will always be for the greater glory of God. Amen.

(Memory)   "Spiritual Battle"
(Intellect)   "Heaven's Help"
(Will)   "St. Michael's Prayer"

Day 7 2.3–2.4 GOOD ANGELS BATTLE
The Bad Angels: (Revelation 12)

Let us take a moment to recall that we are with the Angels in the presence of God and pray: "Dear God, I beg You to please give me the grace, to SPEAK to the three powers of my soul, so my memory, my intellect, and my will, will be for the greater Glory of God."

MEMORY: We see a huge Angel named Michael. He is about eight feet tall and has large wings. He has a sword in his hand that gives off light. We see a battle with the good Angels and the bad Angels. **Michael** and **his Angels** fought with the dragon who is the Devil and Satan (see Revelation 12:7–9).

Behold, a great sign appeared in the sky, a Woman clothed with the sun, the moon under Her feet and on Her head a crown of twelve stars (Revelation 12:1–2). The (Devil) was angry with the Woman, and went to make war with the rest of Her (children) who keep the commandments of God and have the testimony of Jesus Christ (Revelation 12:17).

As can be seen (in Revelation 12:1-2), Mary is wearing a crown on Her head. We see the peaceful look on Mary's face as She wears the crown.

INTELLECT: Why is Mary crowned? What does the crown symbolize? (see Luke 1:38). "He who exalts himself shall be humbled, and he who humbles himself shall be exalted" (Matthew 23:12).

It is Mary's humility that enables Her to know for certain that the "battle is the Lords." This is the root of Her great peace. The Church teaches that God gave Her the crown and She is rightfully called the Queen of Heaven.

2.3 WILL: Angel members will embrace Mary as their Mother and Queen. The Queen Mother will help us apply the graces Jesus Christ obtained for our souls.

MEMORY: We recall that around the world, there have been many apparitions of the Woman clothed with the sun and a crown of twelve stars around Her head in which our Queen has asked us to pray the Rosary every day. God sent Her to tell us over and over to pray, pray, pray, especially the Rosary.

INTELLECT: Why is our Queen Mother asking us to pray and meditate upon the Rosary every day? The Rosary is the weapon against the Devil. The Rosary will defeat the Devil in a way similar to David's sling that defeated Goliath. The five smooth stones David picked up to be used in his sling prefigured the true weapon made up with five decades of the Rosary (see 1 Samuel 17). In order to help imagine this, hold your Rosary from the cross with the loop of beads dangling below it and you will see David's sling. Remember, the fruit of the first mystery is humility. God is going to use the humility of the Blessed Mother to crush the proud head of Satan. The Queen of the Angels has been asking us and teaching us how to pray the Rosary.

The New Catechism of the Catholic Church states that Christian prayer tries, above all, to meditate on the mysteries of Christ, as in the Holy Rosary (#2708). Jesus not only points out the way, "He is the Way". Watch and learn!

2.4 WILL: Angel Members will not fight that battle with fear, violence, or accusations. We will meditate and pray the Rosary as a weapon against Satan. The wisdom of God will inspire Angel Members with truth and grace. As David said, "The battle is the Lord's" (1 Samuel 17:47).

STOP: Take a five minute flight with the Angel. You know what to do.

CLOSE THE FIVE MINUTES BY SAYING . . .
Dear God, I thank You for giving me the grace to SPEAK to the three powers of my soul, so my memory, my intellect, and my will—will always be for the greater glory of God. Amen.

(Memory)	"David's Sling"
(Intellect)	"Spiritual Weapon"
(Will)	"Pray Rosary"

Day 8 3.1–3.2 AN ANGEL HELPS JESUS
During the Agony in the Garden (Luke 22)

Let us take a moment to recall that we are with the Angels in the presence of God and pray: "Dear God, I beg You to please give me the grace, to SPEAK to the three powers of my soul, so my memory, my intellect, and my will, will be for the greater Glory of God."

MEMORY: It is a very dark, damp night. We feel the cool air and hear the crickets chirping. We see the outline of Jesus, who is kneeling by a large rock. His hands are clenched in prayer. He is looking up to His Father in Heaven but is very distressed. We see Jesus's face. He is in agony. Jesus knows He has to suffer to atone for the sins of the world. He walks back to His friends for some support and companionship. "Jesus came to His disciples only to find them asleep exhausted with grief." Jesus wakes them up and then returns by the rock to pray. We see a small light next to Jesus. The light gets larger and brighter. The light takes the form of a beautiful Angel. "An **Angel** appeared to Jesus to strengthen Him. Jesus began to pray even more earnestly, and His sweat became as drops of blood falling down to the ground" (Luke 22:43–44). We see the drops of blood continue to come out of Jesus's forehead. We hear His agonizing pleas to the Father.

INTELLECT: Why was the Angel near Jesus? What did the Angel do for Jesus? The Angel strengthened Jesus so He could pray more fervently. How do we imitate the Angel? The Church is the Mystical Body of Christ. We are many members of one Body (see 1 Cor. 12). The Angel appeared to Jesus in His last day before the crucifixion, to strengthen Him so He could pray more earnestly. Similarly, the Angels of the New Era appear in these Last Days/ New Era to strengthen the Mystical Body of Christ (the Church who is in agony) so its people might pray more fervently to become more united to God.

3.1 WILL: Therefore, Angel members will both participate in prayer groups and promote new prayer groups. Rosary prayer groups will greatly strengthen the whole Church.

MEMORY: We see a band of people come to arrest Jesus. We see Judas kiss Jesus. We see a man grab Jesus. We see Peter use a sword to cut off the servant of the priest's right ear. We hear Jesus say, "Put away your sword, for everyone who lives by the sword, will die by the sword. Don't you know, I can ask My Father, and He will give Me more than **twelve legions of Angels?** How then should the scriptures be fulfilled?" (Matthew 22:52–54).

INTELLECT: Does Jesus use violence or approve of using violence to bring about His Kingdom? God can do everything and does not need our help to accomplish His Holy Will. In His infinite mercy, wisdom, and kindness, God is giving us opportunities to help.

3.2 WILL: Angel members will never use violence as a means of helping Jesus's Kingdom come upon Earth. We must help God in God's way, in peaceful ways, utilizing God's grace, faith, patience, obedience, sacrifice, and mental prayer.

STOP: Take a five-minute flight with the Angel by putting yourself in his place. Make a picture in your mind, and look at the faces.

Use the three powers of your soul: your Memory to ask, **"What do I see? What do I hear? What do I feel? What do I smell?"** Use your Intellect to analyze, **"Why and how?"** and then your Will to make a resolution in your life. For the greater glory of God.

CLOSE THE FIVE MINUTES BY SAYING . . .
Dear God, I thank You for giving me the grace to SPEAK to the three powers of my soul, so my memory, my intellect, and my will—will always be for the greater glory of God. Amen.

(Memory)   "Sweat Blood"
(Intellect)   "Help Pray"
(Will)   "Prayer group"

Day 9 4.1-4.3 ANGELS HELPING
At the Resurrection of Jesus (Matthew 28)

Let us take a moment to recall that we are with the
Angels in the presence of God and pray: "Dear God,
I beg You to please give me the grace, to SPEAK to the
three powers of my soul, so my memory, my intellect,
and my will, will be for the greater Glory of God."

MEMORY: We are with the women disciples outside the gates of the city of Jerusalem. We see the faces of the guards watching Jesus's tomb. It is early morning. The first rays of sunlight are beginning to shine. The birds are chirping. The dew makes everything seem new and fresh. We see a light that comes from the sky and falls to the earth.

Behold, there was a great earthquake for an **Angel** of the Lord descended from Heaven, rolled back the stone and sat upon it. And for fear of Him, the guards were struck with terror and became as dead men. The **Angel** said to the women: "Fear not, for I know you seek Jesus who was crucified. He is not here, for He has risen as He said. Come and see the place where they laid Him" (Matthew 28:1–7). We see the dignified look on the Angel's face as his words echo in our memory. "Fear not, I know you seek Jesus. Be not afraid."

INTELLECT: How can we imitate the Angel? Why does he say "Be not afraid"? Because God is good, Jesus is risen because He is God, and He wants to give us good things.

4.1 WILL: Once again, Angel members will spread the call to "Be not afraid" and to announce the good news that Jesus is alive which will restore faith.

MEMORY: We see the Angel roll the stone away and sit upon it. We look at the Angel's face as he sits on the stone.

INTELLECT: How do we imitate the Angel? Like the stone of the tomb, there are many obstacles such as stones between Jesus and the people. With the prayer of the Angel members, God will soften stony hearts, remove obstacles and restore faith to the people.

Jesus was inside the dark tomb when the Angel rolled the stone away. Several members of the Church find themselves in darkness and confusion. How can we help? We can help by promoting mental prayer.

4.2 WILL: The mental prayer of Angel members will roll the stone away and make us free in the Light of Jesus Christ.

MEMORY: We see the Angel sitting on the stone after he rolled it away.

INTELLECT: Why did the Angel sit on the stone? The Angel was not in a hurry to leave but rolled the stone away and sat upon it. He sat and watched the mystery unfold. He saw the woman. He saw Peter and John running to the tomb. This scene is one of the mysteries of the Rosary.

4.3 WILL: Angel members will also watch the mysteries of the Rosary unfold with mental prayer. Especially, "The Lord is Risen!" will then become a part of the soul's memory. Angel members will also take care not to sit and watch bad shows on TV or movies nor listen to sin-inducing music, which will also become part of our eternal soul's memory. Angel members will want to have their souls give glory to God alone.

STOP: Take a five minute flight with the Angel You know what to do.

(Memory) "Sitting Angel"
(Intellect) "Watch Scene"
(Will)   "Meditate with Rosary"

Day 10 4.4 ANGELS HELPING
At the Resurrection of Jesus (Matthew 28)

Let us take a moment to recall that we are with the Angels in the presence of God and pray: "Dear God, I beg You to please give me the grace, to SPEAK to the three powers of my soul, so my memory, my intellect, and my will, will be for the greater Glory of God."

MEMORY: We are with the women disciples outside the gates of the city of Jerusalem. We see the faces of the guards watching Jesus's tomb. It is early morning. The first rays of sunlight are beginning to shine. The birds are chirping. The dew makes everything seem new and fresh. We see a light descend from Heaven to the earth.

Behold, there was a great earthquake. For an **Angel** of the Lord descended from Heaven and coming rolled back the stone and sat upon it . . . and for fear of him, the guards were struck with terror and became as dead men. The **Angel** said to the women: "Fear not, for I know you seek Jesus who was crucified. He is not here, for He has risen as He said. Come and see the place where they laid Him" (Matthew 28:1–7). We see the astonished look in Mary Magdalene's face as the Angel says, "Go tell his disciples and Peter." The words of the Angel to Mary Magdalene echo over and over, "Go tell His disciples and Peter . . ."

INTELLECT: Why is the Angel saying Peter's name?

As the Angel recognizes and singles out Peter as the head of the disciples, Angel members will recognize the successor of Peter, the Pope, as the head of the Church. After all, Jesus Christ did give Peter the keys to the kingdom of Heaven in a very clear way described in Matthew 16:16–19. Remember, every organization has a visible leader who can make decisions or else there would be total chaos. Does not a ship have a captain? Does not, a school have a principal? A team has a coach? A company has a boss? Our country has a President? When Jesus Christ formed His Church, He made Peter the first Pope, His visible representative on Earth. Pope John Paul II was the 263rd successor of Peter. Pope Benedict XVI is the 264th successor. Pope Francis is the 265th successor. Read Matthew chapter 16 and ask, "How could Jesus have made it more clear?" Christians were united in following the Pope for over the first one thousand years of Christianity. Did Jesus come back and say, "I changed My mind, give Me back the keys"? No way! We need this leadership for unity. Jesus made it clear that, "Every kingdom divided against itself, shall be made desolate" (Matthew 12:25)

4.4 WILL: When it comes to matters of faith and morals, Angel members will follow the authentic Pope. This gives glory to God through Jesus Christ and the Church He built.

STOP: Take a five minute flight with the Angel by putting yourself in his place. Make a picture in your mind, and look at the faces.

Use the three powers of your soul: your Memory to ask, **"What do I see? What do I hear? What do I feel? What do I smell?"** Use your Intellect to analyze, **"Why and how?"** and then your Will to make a resolution in your life all for the greater glory of God.

CLOSE THE FIVE MINUTES BY SAYING . . .
Dear God, I thank You for giving me the grace to SPEAK to the three powers of my soul, so my memory, my intellect, and my will—will always be for the greater glory of God. Amen.

(Memory)   "Peter"

(Intellect)   "Leadership"

(Will)   "Follow Pope"

Day 11 5.1 THE ANGEL'S MISSION
In the Garden of Eden (Genesis 2:1–3:24)

Let us take a moment to recall that we are with the Angels in the presence of God and pray: "Dear God, I beg You to please give me the grace, to SPEAK to the three powers of my soul, so my memory, my intellect, and my will, will be for the greater Glory of God."

MEMORY: We see the peaceful and content look on Adam and Eve in Paradise. They are enjoying absolute freedom living in the state of original justice and happiness. We hear the multitude of birds chirping in harmony. We smell the fragrance of the various flowers as the gentle breeze changes directions. We see Eve take a walk, enjoying the beauty of God's creation. We see the Serpent slither close to her. We hear Eve say, "we cannot even touch it or we shall die" (Genesis 3:3). We hear the Serpent trick Eve and accuse God. We see them eat the forbidden fruit from the tree. We see their faces lose their peace and now filled with anxiety and fear. We see them hide from God.

Almost everyone knows that Adam and Eve ate the forbidden fruit. However, there was not only one special tree in the Garden of Eden, but two: the forbidden Tree of Knowledge and the good Tree of Life. The Devil tricked Adam and Eve into breaking their covenant with God and eating the forbidden fruit, for which the punishment was to die the death.

Then God said, "Behold Adam is become as one of us knowing good and evil: now, therefore, lest perhaps he put forth his hand and take also of the Tree of Life, and eat and live forever." And the Lord sent him out of the paradise of pleasure, to till the earth from which he was taken. And He cast out Adam; and placed before the paradise of pleasure **Cherubim [Angels]**, and a flaming sword, turning every way, to keep the way of the Tree of Life (Genesis 3:22–24).

INTELLECT: The first mission of the Angels recorded in the Bible is to keep the path of the Tree of Life. This is also our mission. Most people do not know where the path is. The Fruit of this Tree is the antidote which will allow us to live forever. The fulfillment to the True Tree of Life is the Blessed Virgin Mary, the Cross, and the Holy Catholic Church. These truths will be manifested to you by the Holy Spirit as you pray the Rosary. A great clue to finding this Tree is revealed during the Visitation of Mary to Her cousin Elizabeth. Elizabeth filled with the Holy Spirit said, "Blessed art thou among women, and Blessed is the FRUIT of Thy womb." The Fruit of the Tree of Life is the Fruit of Her womb, Jesus Christ, the second person of the Blessed Trinity; specifically Holy Communion, which is also known as the Eucharist. This is why the Blessed Virgin Mary is the true Tree of Life.

The Eucharist is Jesus Christ, our God here for us, under the appearance of bread. Jesus Christ makes it very, very clear that we are to eat Holy Communion to live forever. [In the second half of John 6] Jesus said, "He that eats My flesh and drinks My Blood lives in Me and I in him" (John 6:57), and "he that eats this Bread will live forever" (John 6:59). The Blood means that Jesus Christ is alive. Jesus is God, and He can live inside of us invisibly if he wanted to. Jesus decided to live inside of us when we make an effort to prepare ourselves and receive Him through His special miracle of the Eucharist. When Jesus first gave us Holy Communion at the Last Supper, He also made it clear that this is the NEW COVENANT between God and His people. Just as an apple hangs from the wood of the tree, Jesus Christ hung from the wood of the Cross. By a miracle, the time period from Holy Thursday to Easter Sunday including the Crucifixion is made present at every Mass. This is why the Cross is also the Tree of Life.

We physically go to the Holy Catholic Church to receive Holy Communion. This is why the members of the Church and especially, the priesthood are also the Tree of Life and the fruit once again is Jesus Christ. The Eucharistic Covenant between God and His people is most important. As we travel into the third millennium, polls show that ONLY TWENTY PERCENT OF CATHOLICS in America under the age of 50 understand the importance of Holy Communion. This means that eighty percent are completely lost and confused about their covenant with God. ANGEL MEMBERS HAVE A BIG JOB

TO DO. Imagine that eighty percent of the players on a basketball team did not know it was important to score a basket. How many games would they win? Similarly, [with such confusion] the people of God will continue to lose all spiritual battles. Of course, when Angel members evangelize the life giving fruit of the Eucharist, we will point out the necessity of getting the soul into the state of grace with the sacrament of Confession.

5.1 WILL: Angel members will keep the path of the Tree of Life by evangelizing the life-giving fruit of the Eucharist, Jesus, from the Tree of the Blessed Mother, the Cross, and the Church.

STOP: Take a five minute flight with the Angel. You know what to do.

(Memory)   "Tree of Life"
(Intellect)   "Antidote–Live forever"
(Will)   "Evangelize Eucharist"

Day 12 1.3–1.4 ANGELS OF CHRISTMAS
Jesus's Birthday (Luke 2:1–16)

Let us take a moment to recall that we are with the Angels in the presence of God and pray: "Dear God, I beg You to please give me the grace, to SPEAK to the three powers of my soul, so my memory, my intellect, and my will, will be for the greater Glory of God."

MEMORY: We are with the shepherds in the fields. We see the bright stars twinkling on a clear night. We feel the cold air, and we hear the crickets and the sheep bleating in the distance. We smell burnt wood from the fire that was made to keep us warm. We look up. A light in the sky gets very bright. The light takes the form of a beautiful Angel. The Angel has a soft glow around his white wings. We become afraid of the unusual but magnificent sight. His voice was young, but powerful as if it echoed all the way back up to heaven.

We recall the **Angel of the Lord** appeared to the shepherds and said, "Be not afraid, I bring you tidings of great joy [good news] which shall be shared to all the people; for today in the town of David, a Savior is born to you who is Christ the Lord" (Luke 2:10-11).

We hear heavenly sounds. The soothing music gets louder as the melody and harmony is added. We see the brightness of the Angel increase. Suddenly there was with the **Angel** a multitude of the **Heavenly**

army, praising God and saying, **"Glory to God in the highest and peace on Earth to people of good will"** (Luke 2:13–14). We look at the face of a shepherd. What do we see? The words of the Angel echo in our memory "Glory to God in the highest and peace on Earth to people of good will."

INTELLECT: Why are the Angels who are praising God, telling them to have peace on Earth, to give glory to God, and to have good will? How can we imitate the Angels? The Angels are letting us know the formula to obtain true peace: Praise God, have good will, and give glory to God. This formula is contained in the Angels of the New Era vow. We will both repeat the vow and encourage others to pray it also.

1.3 WILL: A multitude of Angel members will be imitating the heavenly army by repeating the Angels vow. The vow is, "We promise to beg God for the grace that the three powers of our soul, my memory, my intellect, and my will, will be for the greater glory of God." We will both repeat the vow and encourage others to pray it also. In this way, we imitate the Heavenly army present at Jesus's birth.

MEMORY: We hear the Angel say, "Peace on Earth to people of good will." The words of the Angel echo in our memory, "Peace on Earth to people of good will." Why is the Angel saying this?

INTELLECT: What does good will mean? Good will means to keep trying to please God more than pleasing yourself. Peace is a gift that can only come from God. You cannot have joy without peace.

1.4 WILL: No matter what kind of sinner you are, keep trying to please God and you will obtain peace.

STOP: Take a five minute flight with the Angel by putting yourself in his place. Make a picture in your mind, and look at the faces.

Use the three powers of your soul: your Memory to ask, **"What do I see? What do I hear? What do I feel? What do I smell?"** Use your Intellect to analyze, **"Why and how?"** and then your Will to make a resolution in your life all for the greater glory of God.

CLOSE THE FIVE MINUTES by saying . . .

Dear God, I thank You for giving me the grace to SPEAK to the three powers of my soul, so my memory, my intellect, and my will—will always be for the greater glory of God. Amen.

(Memory)	"Peace"
(Intellect)	"Have Good will"
(Will)	"Please God"

Day 13 1.5 ANGELS OF CHRISTMAS
Jesus's Birthday (Luke 2:1–16)

Let us take a moment to recall that we are with the Angels in the presence of God and pray: "Dear God, I beg You to please give me the grace, to SPEAK to the three powers of my soul, so my memory, my intellect, and my will, will be for the greater Glory of God."

MEMORY: What do I see? What do I hear? What do I feel? What do I smell?

We are with the shepherds in the fields. We see the bright stars twinkling on a clear night. We feel the cold air, and we hear the crickets and the sheep bleating in the distance.

We hear heavenly music and we see the brightness of the Angel increase. Suddenly, there was with the **Angel** a multitude of the **Heavenly army** praising God and saying: **"Glory to God in the highest and peace on Earth to people of good will"** (Luke 2:13-14).

The multitude of the Heavenly Angels praised God and as in the Book of Revelation repeated, "Hosanna, Hosanna, Hosanna! Holy, Holy, Holy!" (Luke 2:13, Revelation 4:8). We look at the expression of the Angel's face. The words of the Angel echo in our memory, "Hosanna, Hosanna, Hosanna! Hosanna, Hosanna, Hosanna!"

INTELLECT: Why are the Angels repeating their praises to God? How can we imitate them? The Angels have a pure love for God. Love is the key factor in prayer! If you make a repeating noise with your lips and do not pray with the heart, then it is vain repetition. It is love that differentiates a repeated prayer from vain repetition and makes it a powerful spiritual exercise. Repeating push-ups can build muscles in your body. Praying with the heart will build up your soul.

1.5 WILL: The Angel members will repeat prayers with love.

STOP: Take a five minute flight with the Angel by putting yourself in his place. Make a picture in your mind, and look at the faces.

CLOSE THE FIVE MINUTES by saying . . .

Dear God, I thank You for giving me the grace to SPEAK to the three powers of my soul, so my memory, my intellect, and my will—will always be for the greater glory of God. Amen.

(Memory)	"Holy, Holy, Holy"
(Intellect)	"Spiritual exercise"
(Will)	"Repeat praise"

Day 14 6.6 ANGEL GABRIEL'S ANNUNCIATION To Mary: (Luke 1:26–38)

Let us take a moment to recall that we are with the Angels in the presence of God and pray: "Dear God, I beg You to please give me the grace, to SPEAK to the three powers of my soul, so my memory, my intellect, and my will, will be for the greater Glory of God."

MEMORY: We see the three persons in God, the Father, the Son and the Holy Spirit looking over poor humanity on Earth engaged in violence and bad language. God sees that many souls are on the road to Hell. However, God smiles at what He sees in a small, humble house. It is Mary. She is about fifteen years old. She has black hair, blue eyes, and rosy cheeks. She smiles as She sews a blanket. Although She is working on Earth, Her heart is thinking of God in Heaven. God then says, "It is time," and dispatches an Angel. We see Angel Gabriel. He is dressed in white. He has large wings. There is a glow of white that surrounds him. We think of purity.

The Angel **Gabriel** was sent by God, to a city of Galilee called Nazareth to a Virgin espoused to a man named Joseph, of the house of David, and the Virgin's name was Mary. And the **Angel** came in and said to Her, "Hail, full of grace, the Lord is with thee, blessed art thou among women" (Luke 1:26–28). We see the beautiful Angel say, "Hail, Full of Grace, the Lord is with You. Blessed are You."

INTELLECT: We ask, "How did this change Mary?"

Before the Annunciation of the Angel Gabriel, God lived in Mary by grace. After the Annunciation, Jesus, Who is God made Flesh, physically lived inside of the Blessed Virgin Mary. Today, we see many souls are on the road to Hell. How is God going to change this? God sends His Angel members to imitate Gabriel and evangelize the people that God made Flesh wants to live inside of them. They are to love Him. God will change their hearts, and in this way, the world will be changed.

6.6 WILL: Angel members will encourage people to give their total yes to God and prepare themselves to welcome Jesus so He can live inside of them. Angel members will remember these things about the Hail Mary.

HAIL: This is a humble respectful greeting. Angel members must be full of humility and respect in order to evangelize. Arrogance will greatly minimize evangelization efforts.

FULL OF GRACE: Angel members must tell them, that in order to receive the living God in their bodies, their souls must be in a state of grace. The Sacrament of Confession is the means Jesus gave us to restore our souls to a state of grace.

THE LORD IS WITH YOU: Emmanuel, God is with us and loves us. This is the Good News.

BLESSED ARE YOU: There is no greater way to build up our treasure in Heaven than when Jesus is living inside of us.

STOP: Take a five minute flight with the Angel. You know what to do.

(Memory)   "Jesus in Mary"
(Intellect)   "Change the world"
(Will)   "Jesus in us"

Day 15 6.7–6.9 ANGEL GABRIEL'S ANNUNCIATION To Mary: (Luke 1:26–38)

Let us take a moment to recall that we are with the Angels in the presence of God and pray: "Dear God, I beg You to please give me the grace, to SPEAK to the three powers of my soul, so my memory, my intellect, and my will, will be for the greater Glory of God."

MEMORY: We see the three persons in God, the Father, the Son and the Holy Spirit looking over poor humanity on Earth engaged in violence and bad language. God sees that many souls are on the road to Hell. However, God smiles at what He sees in a small, humble house. It is Mary. She is about fifteen years old. She has black hair, blue eyes, and rosy cheeks. She smiles as She sews a blanket. Although She is working on Earth, Her heart is thinking of God in Heaven. God then says, "It is time," and dispatches an Angel. We see Angel Gabriel. He is dressed in white. He has large wings. There is a glow of white that surrounds him.

The **Angel Gabriel** was sent by God to a city of Galilee called Nazareth to a Virgin espoused to a man named Joseph, of the house of David, and the Virgin's name was Mary. And the **Angel** came in and said to her, "Hail, full of grace, the Lord is with Thee, blessed art Thou among women" (Luke 1:26–28). The Angel said to Her, "Fear not, Mary, for thou has found grace with God" (Luke 1:30). We look at Mary's face as we hear the Angel say, "Fear not Mary, for thou has found grace with God" (Luke 1:30).

INTELLECT: How can we listen to and imitate the Angel?

6.7 WILL: Once again Angel members will "be not afraid" and convey the message to "be not afraid." Do not be afraid of being holy. God calls everyone to be holy, because He is Holy.

MEMORY: We hear the Angel say, "Behold, Thou shall conceive in the womb and bring forth a son; and call Him Jesus. He shall be great, and be called the Son of the most High" (Luke 1:31-32).

INTELLECT: How is Jesus going to begin His journey on Earth?

The Angel lets us know that Jesus's first entrance into the world was as a slave of love to the Blessed Mother. The Mighty God inside Her womb would go only where Mary went. This helps us to understand Jesus's slavery of love to us in Holy Communion. For fifteen minutes after Holy Communion, Jesus physically lives in us as He lived inside the Blessed Mother.

6.8 WILL: Angel members will love Jesus living in us the way Mary did, with Her whole heart. We will make an effort to receive Jesus in Holy Communion with Love.

MEMORY: We see that Jesus is living inside of Mary and only goes where She carries Him.

INTELLECT: Jesus was not only a slave of love in Mary for nine months. It gave glory to God that He was subject to Mary and Joseph for thirty years before the three and one third years of His public ministry.

Doing a consecration to Jesus through Mary, one receives tremendous amounts of grace as he imitates Jesus to be a holy slave of love to God through the Blessed Virgin Mary. Pope John Paul II's motto was "Totus Tuus" or "Totally Yours." This motto comes from Saint Louis DeMontfort's consecration. He stumbled upon this True Devotion and found it to be very Christocentric. Think about his short time between working in the soda factory and becoming Pope. It is truly phenomenal. Mother Theresa of Calcutta has the fastest growing order of Sisters in the history of the Catholic Church, and she recommends to all novices to practice Total Consecration and to spend one hour a day in Eucharistic Adoration. It is an easy, short, sure, and safe way of obtaining union with our Lord.

6.9 WILL: Angel members are highly recommended to practice Saint Louis DeMontfort's Total Consecration.

STOP: Take a five minute flight with the Angel.

Use the three powers of your soul: your Memory to ask, **"What do I see? What do I hear? What do I feel? What do I smell?"** Use your Intellect to analyze, **"Why and how?"** and then your Will to make a resolution in your life all for the greater glory of God.

(Memory)	"Jesus in Mary"
(Intellect)	"Imitate Jesus"
(Will)	"Us in Mary"

Day 16 9.1–9.2 ANGELS REJOICE
For the Conversion of Sinners: (Luke 15:4–10)

Let us take a moment to recall that we are with the Angels in the presence of God and pray: "Dear God, I beg You to please give me the grace, to SPEAK to the three powers of my soul, so my memory, my intellect, and my will, will be for the greater Glory of God."

MEMORY: We hear the hundred sheep bleating. We feel the warm dry air of the desert. We see a flock of sheep. We see a man carrying a sheep on his shoulders returning to the flock. We see the big smile on his face.

Jesus said, "What man among you that has a hundred sheep, and if he shall lose one of them, does he not leave the ninety-nine in the desert, and go after that which was lost until he finds it. And when he has found it, lay it upon his shoulders rejoicing: coming home, calls together his friends and neighbors saying to them: 'Rejoice with me, because I have found the sheep that was lost?' I say to you, that even so, there shall be joy in Heaven upon one sinner that does penance, more than upon the ninety-nine just who need not penance" (Luke 15:4–7). "Or what woman having ten coins, if she loses one, does not light a candle, and sweep the house, and seek diligently until she finds it? And when she has found it, calls together her friends and neighbors saying; 'Rejoice with me, because I have found the coin which I had lost.' So I say to you there shall be joy before the **Angels of God** upon one sinner doing penance" (Luke 15:8–10). We see the joy on the Angel's face.

INTELLECT: Why are the Angels so joyful upon one sinner doing penance and how do we imitate them? Love wants everyone to be in Heaven someday.

9.1 WILL: Angel members must always be joyful over conversions. God's love is infinite and has enough love for everyone. Never be jealous or envious. Remember the book of Wisdom states, "Through envy of the Devil, death entered into the world" (Wisdom 2:24). Quench any ill feelings with a bucket of thanksgiving and joy. Give glory to God always.

MEMORY: We see a man smiling as he carries a sheep on his shoulders, and we hear the Angels rejoicing.

INTELLECT: How does this parable apply to our faith?
Jesus represents the man in the parable because He is the Good Shepherd who lays His life down for His sheep. Mary, our Queen, represents the Woman in the parable who, through all the apparitions in the world, is diligently looking for Her lost children and converting them back to Jesus.

9.2 WILL: Once again, Angel members will rejoice for conversions and help Jesus and Mary find them and bring them back home.

STOP: Take a five minute flight with the Angel.

Use the three powers of your soul: your Memory to ask, **"What do I see? What do I hear? What do I feel? What do I smell?"** Use your Intellect to analyze, **"Why and how?"** and then your Will to make a resolution in your life all for the greater glory of God.

(Memory)   "Angel's rejoicing"
(Intellect)   "Rejoice for Conversions"
(Will)   "Fight envy"

Day 17 7.1–7.2 ANGELS MINISTER
After the Temptation in the Desert: (Matth. 4.1–11)

Let us take a moment to recall that we are with the Angels in the presence of God and pray: "Dear God, I beg You to please give me the grace, to SPEAK to the three powers of my soul, so my memory, my intellect, and my will, will be for the greater Glory of God."

MEMORY: We see Jesus in the desert. He looks thin because He just fasted for forty days. We feel the warm dry air. We hear the wind whistling through the rocky cliffs. We hear a vulture call at a distance. We see the Devil in the appearance of a man tempting Jesus to turn stones into bread. We hear Jesus say to the Devil, "Not on bread alone does man live, but on every word that comes from the mouth of God." We see the Devil take Him to the Holy City and set Jesus on the pinnacle of the Temple. He says, "If thou art the Son of God, cast yourself down. For it is written 'He has given His Angels charge over you, and in their hands they shall bear you up, lest perhaps You dash Your foot against a stone' Jesus said to him: 'It is written again' Thou shalt not tempt the Lord thy God'" After Jesus was tempted in the desert, the **Angels** came to minister to Him (Matthew 4:4–11). We notice the eagerness on the Angels' faces as they minister to Jesus.

INTELLECT: How do we imitate the Angels? The Angels came to minister to Jesus. Angel members will always have mercy on those persons who are being tempted by the Devil. The things that tempted persons need the most are prayers and love. This will help them to overcome the attack. Only after the attack is over, will they be capable of fully receiving the Lord's Word to help them live as children of God.

7.1 WILL: Angel members will help people being tempted by the Devil with love, prayers, sacrifice, and encouragement.

MEMORY: We see the Devil tempting Jesus.

INTELLECT: How do we become aware of the tricks of bad Angels? Note that in the supernatural battle, the Devil himself used Scripture to try to trick Jesus. The Devil said, "If you are the Son of God, cast yourself down, for it is written . . ." (Deuteronomy 8:3, Matthew 4:6). Jesus exposes the trick by showing that the Devil took the quote out of context. This means that the Devil takes a few words and gives them a meaning that they do not really have. The enemy of your soul can use this to slow down your personal conversion.

7.2 WILL: Know this, Angel Members: when someone quotes Scripture and you feel it paralyze your soul, the enemy is attacking. Remind them that

Jesus Christ did not give us a Bible. He gave us an Apostolic Church guided by the Holy Spirit. God used His holy, Catholic Church, guided by the Holy Spirit, to give us the Bible. God gave that same Church, guided by the Holy Spirit, the correct interpretations of the Bible.

As you pray the Scriptural Rosary, you will be rooted in learning the Bible in context, and also be filled with the Holy Spirit in order to handle attacks more effectively. This takes time.

STOP: Take a five minute flight with the Angel.

You know what to do.

(Memory)   "Devil's tricks"
(Intellect)   "Misuse Scripture"
(Will)   "Scripture Rosary"

Day 18 7.3–7.4 ANGELS MINISTER
After the Temptation in the Desert: (Matth 4.1–11)

Let us take a moment to recall that we are with the Angels in the presence of God and pray: "Dear God, I beg You to please give me the grace, to SPEAK to the three powers of my soul, so my memory, my intellect, and my will, will be for the greater Glory of God."

MEMORY: We see Jesus in the desert. He looks thin because He just fasted for forty days. We feel the warm dry air. We hear the wind whistling through the rocky cliffs. We hear a vulture call at a distance. We see the Devil in the appearance of a man tempting Jesus to turn stones into bread. We hear Jesus say to the Devil, "Not on bread alone does man live, but on every word that comes from the mouth of God." We see the Devil take Him to the Holy City and set Jesus on the pinnacle of the Temple. He says, "If thou art the Son of God, cast yourself down. For it is written 'He has given His Angels charge over you, and in their hands they shall bear you up, lest perhaps You dash Your foot against a stone' Jesus said to him: 'It is written again' Thou shalt not tempt the Lord thy God'" After Jesus was tempted in the desert, the **Angels** came to minister to Him (Matthew 4:4–11). We notice the eagerness on the Angels' faces as they minister to Jesus.

MEMORY: We hear the Devil using scripture to tempt Jesus. We hear Jesus explain the scriptures in context.

INTELLECT: A good example of this is the use of statues. Some people who do not understand mental prayer may lash out and say, "Catholics should not be worshipping statues." Check the new Catechism and find that, in fact, Catholics do not worship statues.

If someone does, there is something wrong. Scriptures IN CONTEXT shows that God even commanded the Israelites to **make statues of Angels** (Cherubim) to put on the "ARK of the Covenant" (Exodus 25:18). Statues are excellent tools for creating an environment of mental prayer. For example, ask the person to take a picture of a loved one out of their wallet. As they look at it, they will smile because their **memory** will help them recall good times. Ask them if they think the picture is a real person. They will reply, "Of course not, but the picture helps me remember them, when I can't see them face to face." Continue and ask them, "Do you think the statue of Abraham Lincoln in the Lincoln Memorial is a god?" They will again reply, "Of course not, the statue just reminds us of a great president who promoted honesty and self-sacrifice to serve the country." Then explain to them, statues help the memory, which is one of the three powers of the soul to focus. For example, "Statues of Joseph, Mary and the baby Jesus remind us of the wonderful story of Christmas. If we do not have statues as a tool for reminding us and helping us to meditate more deeply on Christmas, we may get caught up in materialism and forget the Holy Family completely."

7.3 WILL: All misunderstandings or Scriptures taken out of context that are against the Holy Catholic Church can easily be explained with the help of the Holy Spirit, mental prayer, and the *Catechism of the Catholic Church*. Angel members will become familiar with these holy tools.

7.4 WILL: Remember Angel members: the Devil did not argue with Jesus because he wanted to know the truth. He only wanted to make Jesus fall into sin. Sometimes it is better not to argue and just walk away. Call on the Holy Spirit and your guardian Angel to guide you.

STOP: Take a five minute flight with the Angel. You know what to do.

(Memory)	"Devil's tricks"
(Intellect)	"Out of context"
(Will)	"Catechism Catholic Church"

Day 19 8.1–8.2 THE ANGEL RELEASES PETER from Prison (Acts 12:1–19)

Let us take a moment to recall that we are with the Angels in the presence of God and pray: "Dear God, I beg You to please give me the grace, to SPEAK to the three powers of my soul, so my memory, my intellect, and my will, will be for the greater Glory of God."

MEMORY: We see persecution against the Christians.

"Herod killed James the brother of John with the sword" (Acts 12:2). He cast Peter into prison. We see Peter behind bars. We hear the clank of the chains to his hands and feet. We see two guards at the door. We see Peter fall asleep as it gets dark. "But prayer was made without ceasing by the Church unto God for him. And behold an Angel of the Lord stood by him: and a light shined in the room: and he striking Peter on the side, raised him up, saying: Arise quickly. And the chains fell off from his hands. And the Angel said to him: Get dressed, and put on thy sandals. And he did so. And he said to him: Put on your coat, and follow me. And going out, he followed him, and he knew not that it was true which was done by the Angel: but thought he saw a vision. And passing through the first and the second ward, they came to the iron gate that leads to the city, which of itself opened to them. And going out, they passed on through one street: and immediately the Angel departed from him. And

Peter coming to himself, said, Now I know in very deed, that the Lord hath sent His Angel, and hath delivered me out of the hand of Herod, and from all the expectation of the people of the Jews" (Acts 12:1–19). We are impressed by how the large chains fell off Peter's hands and the look of astonishment on his face as the iron gate opened for him.

INTELLECT: How is the spiritual life similar to freedom and prison? Jesus once said, "Everyone who sins is a slave to sin" (John 8:34).

The graces obtained by mental prayer will help free us from the slavery of the Devil, and restore us to the people of God. The Angel members' work will promote true freedom.

8.1 WILL: Once again, Angel members will pray for the freedom of people in the slavery of sin, otherwise known as conversions. Angel members will help people with their conversions.

MEMORY: We see the dark jail. We see the chains on Peter. An **Angel** of the Lord stood by him, and a light shined in the room and he, striking Peter on the side, said, "Arise quickly, follow me" (Acts 12:7).

INTELLECT: How do we imitate the Angel? Angel members will be a shining light for people to follow. The path of true freedom leaves the slavery of sin behind and walks in the Light and Love of Jesus Christ. People need good examples to follow.

8.2 WILL: Angel members will always strive to be holy, and have great confidence that God will give them all the graces they need to be holy. They must not only talk the talk but must walk the walk in order to lead many people out of the slavery of sin. This will be a good example to all.

STOP: Take a five minute flight with the Angel. You know what to do.

(Memory)   "Chains"
(Intellect)   "Sin is slavery"
(Will)   "Holy life—freedom"

Day 20 8.3–8.4 THE ANGEL RELEASES PETER from Prison (Acts 12:1–19)

Let us take a moment to recall that we are with the Angels in the presence of God and pray: "Dear God, I beg You to please give me the grace, to SPEAK to the three powers of my soul, so my memory, my intellect, and my will, will be for the greater Glory of God."

MEMORY: We see persecution against the Christians. "Herod killed James the brother of John with the sword" (Acts 12:2). He cast Peter into prison. We see Peter behind bars. We hear the clank of the chains to his hands and feet. We see two guards at the door. We see Peter fall asleep as it gets dark. "But prayer was made without ceasing by the Church unto God for him. And behold an Angel of the Lord stood by him: and a light shined in the room: and he striking Peter on the side, raised him up, saying: Arise quickly. And the chains fell off from his hands. And the Angel said to him: Get dressed, and put on thy sandals. And he did so. And he said to him: Put on your coat, and follow me. And going out, he followed him, and he knew not that it was true which was done by the Angel: but thought he saw a vision. And passing through the first and the second ward, they came to the iron-gate that leads to the city, which of itself opened to them. And going out, they passed on through one street: and immediately the Angel departed from him. And Peter coming to himself, said, Now I know in very deed, that the Lord hath sent His Angel, and hath delivered me out of the hand of Herod, and from all the expectation of the people of the Jews" (Acts 12:1–19). We are attracted to the way all the chains fell and then all the doors opened while Peter followed the Angel.

INTELLECT: Why are there so many obstacles?

Sometimes conversion is a long journey and there are many obstacles to being free, even some that are humanly impossible.

8.3 WILL: Angel members will persevere because God will open up the right doors and nothing will be impossible. Angel members will follow the path of conversion.

MEMORY: We see that Peter is free. There is joy on Peter's face. Peter said, "'Now I know . . . that the Lord sent His **Angel** to deliver me from the hand of Herod' . . . Peter knocked at the gate where many were praying … they opened not the gate . . . But Peter continued knocking" (Acts 12:11–16). We see Peter looking over his shoulder. We hear the knock on the wooden door. We see Peter knocking and knocking. We hear his friends inside whispering, "It can't be Peter, he is in prison." We see the puzzled look on Peter's face as he continues to knock on the door.

INTELLECT: Why did Peter continue knocking? Even Peter's friends were very slow in believing he was free. Today, there may be a similar mystery.

Millions of people are being converted in Medjugorje. There are other people who have specifically been praying for their freedom or conversion, yet they are slow to believe the conversion events are true.

Of course, when dealing with these and all apparitions, we humbly submit to the Vatican's ruling (See section 4.4).

8.4 WILL: Angel members, be patient with those who do not believe in conversion experiences; remember that eventually Peter was welcomed with joy.

STOP: Take a five-minute flight with the Angel. You know what to do.

(Memory)	"Peter knocking"
(Intellect)	"Slow believing"
(Will)	"Patience"

Day 21 6.10 ANGEL GABRIEL'S ANNUNCIATION to Mary: (Luke 1:26–38)

Let us take a moment to recall that we are with the Angels in the presence of God and pray: "Dear God, I beg You to please give me the grace, to SPEAK to the three powers of my soul, so my memory, my intellect, and my will, will be for the greater Glory of God."

MEMORY: We see the three persons in God, the Father, the Son and the Holy Spirit looking over poor humanity engaged in violence and bad language. God sees that many souls are on the road to Hell. However, God smiles at what He sees in a small, humble house. It is Mary. She is about fifteen years old. She has black hair, blue eyes, and rosy cheeks. She smiles, as She sews a blanket. Although She is working on Earth, Her heart is thinking of God in Heaven. God then says, "It is time," and dispatches an Angel. We see Angel Gabriel. He is dressed in white. He has large wings. There is a glow of white that surrounds him. The Angel **Gabriel** was sent by God to a city of Galilee called Nazareth to a Virgin espoused to a man named Joseph, of the house of David, and the Virgin's name was Mary. And the **Angel** came in and said to her, "Hail, full of grace, the Lord is with Thee, blessed art Thou among women" (Luke 1:26–28). The Angel said to Her, "Fear not, Mary, for thou has found grace with God" (Luke 1:30).

We see the Angel in dazzling white, bow before Mary. We hear the Angel say to Mary, "And the Lord will give Him the throne of David His father" (Luke 1:32). These words of the Angel echo over and over in our minds, "The Lord will give Him the throne of David, his Father."

INTELLECT: How did David get his throne?

Just as God gave David his throne by means of the sling he used as the weapon to defeat Goliath, God the Father will have Jesus's Kingdom come about on Earth through His mystical body, the Church, and praying the Rosary as the weapon against evil. As discussed in section 2.4, the Rosary is the weapon that will defeat the evil throne of the Devil. Rosary prayers are the key to bring about Jesus's Kingdom on Earth.

As David went to the brook and pulled out five smooth stones for his sling, there are five decades or smooth stones of the Rosary.
God sent the Blessed Virgin Mary to personally give Saint Dominic the Rosary along with fifteen powerful promises to those who pray the Rosary. Many Popes and Saints throughout the years have affirmed this fact, and the many graces the faithful obtain by praying the Rosary. See Pope Leo XIII's encyclical *Supremi Apostolatus* (1883) and Saint Louis DeMontfort's *Secret of the Rosary*.

The Devil tries to discourage people from praying the Rosary, because he cannot defend himself from it. Pope Pius IX said, where does the power of the Rosary come from? It comes from the meditation on the Gospel lives of Jesus and Mary.

6.10 WILL: Angel members are highly recommended to pray the Rosary often and meditate on its mysteries to help bring about Jesus's reign on Earth.

STOP: Take a five minute flight with the Angel You know what to do.

(Memory)	"Throne David"
(Intellect)	"Conquer"
(Will)	"Pray Rosary"

Day 22 9.3–9.4 ANGELS REJOICE

For the Conversion of Sinners: (Luke 15:4–10)

Let us take a moment to recall that we are with the Angels in the presence of God and pray: "Dear God, I beg You to please give me the grace, to SPEAK to the three powers of my soul, so my memory, my intellect, and my will, will be for the greater Glory of God."

MEMORY: We hear the hundred sheep bleating. We feel the warm dry air of the desert. We see a flock of sheep. We see a man carrying a sheep on his shoulders returning to the flock. We see the big smile on his face.

Jesus said, "What man among you that has a hundred sheep, and if he shall lose one of them, does he not leave the ninety-nine in the desert, and go after that which was lost until he find it. And when he has found it, lay it upon his shoulders rejoicing: coming home, calls together his friends and neighbors saying to them: 'Rejoice with me, because I have found the sheep that was lost?' I say to you, that even so, there shall be joy in Heaven upon one sinner that does penance, more than upon the ninety-nine just who need not penance" (Luke 15:4–7). "Or what woman having ten coins, if she loses one, does not light a candle, and sweep the house, and seek diligently until she find it? And when she has found it, calls together her friends and neighbors saying; 'Rejoice with me, because I have found the coin which I had lost.' So I say to you there shall be joy before the **Angels of God** upon one sinner doing penance" (Luke 15:8–10).

INTELLECT: This parable shows mercy in action. These are the times of great mercy. Saint Sister Mary Faustina received the chaplet of Divine Mercy to pray. He instructed her to practice the A, B, C's of mercy. **A**sk for His mercy, **B**e merciful, and **C**omplete trust. Angel members will benefit abundantly by delivering the message of mercy.

9.3 WILL: With great joy Angel members will practice and promote the Infinite Mercy of God.

MEMORY: We see the happy Angels in Heaven. We hear them rejoicing upon one sinner doing penance.

INTELLECT: How long does it take to be converted? What helps this process?

9.4 WILL: Conversion is a life-long project! Every night, the Angel members are recommended to examine their conscience in light of Jesus's example and repent for any sins they committed during the day. "Take time to read the book of your daily life." God will protect us from external enemies, but He will only *help* protect us from internal ones. We must ask God for the grace to overcome pride, lust, greed, anger, envy, sloth, and gluttony. Ask God to replace these with the fire of His love. Receiving Jesus in Holy Communion and experiencing His

Mercy in frequent Confession helps. Upon doing this, be certain that there is much rejoicing by the **Angels** of God.

STOP: Take a five minute flight with the Angel. You know what to do.

(Memory)	"Angel's rejoicing"
(Intellect)	"Our conversion"
(Will)	"Examine conscience"

Day 23 10.1 TOBIT IS HELPED
By the Angel Raphael: (Tobit 1–14)

Let us take a moment to recall that we are with the Angels in the presence of God and pray: "Dear God, I beg You to please give me the grace, to SPEAK to the three powers of my soul, so my memory, my intellect, and my will, will be for the greater Glory of God."

MEMORY: We see a holy man named Tobit. He is dressed in simple but tidy clothes. Tobit feared God and abstained from sin. He fed the hungry, gave clothes to the naked and was heroic in burying the dead. The Lord permitted Tobit to go blind in order to test his patience like Job. He sent his son Tobit [Jr.] on a long journey to collect ten talents of silver which he lent.

The Lord sent the **Angel Raphael**, who appeared as a person, to accompany Tobit on the journey. We see the **Angel Raphael** and Tobit talking as they walk along the long journey. We see the **Angel Raphael** save Tobit from being devoured by a large fish. We hear the large splash. We hear the **Angel Raphael** advise Tobit to defeat the demon that was oppressing his new wife by praying and fasting. We see Tobit collecting the money. It was a very adventurous and successful trip. When they returned home, the **Angel Raphael** cured Tobit Senior of his blindness. Tobit said, "What can we give to this holy man (the Angel) for traveling with you?" His

son responded, "He traveled with me and brought
me home safe again.

He received the money of Gabelus.
He caused me to have my wife.
He chased from her the evil spirit. He gave joy to her
parents.

Myself he delivered from being devoured by the
fish. You also he has made to see the light of
Heaven. We are filled with all good things through
him" (Tobit 12:3).
For this Tobit and his son intended to give Raphael
half the wealth they obtained. The **Angel Raphael**
said, "Bless God of Heaven, give glory to Him, in
the sight of all that live, because He has shown His
mercy to you. Prayer is good with fasting and alms,
more than to lay up treasures of gold. But they that
commit sin and iniquity are enemies to their own
soul . . . I am the **Angel Raphael**, one of the seven
who stand before the throne of God. Peace be to you
and fear not. When I was with you, it was by the
will of God. Bless Him and sing praise to Him."
Tobit and his family gave glory to God and
prospered.

INTELLECT: We marvel at all the things Raphael
helped Tobit with. How can we imitate the **Angel
Raphael**?

Raphael helped with many corporal works of
Mercy.

10.1 WILL: Angel members will practice and live deeds of mercy (Catechism Catholic Church #2447).

SPIRITUAL WORKS OF MERCY

1. To teach the ignorant
2. To counsel the needy
3. To chastise the sinful
4. To comfort the sorrowful
5. To forgive enemies
6. To suffer tribulation
7. To pray for all fervently

CORPORAL WORKS OF MERCY

1. Feed the hungry
2. Give drink to the thirsty
3. Clothe the naked
4. Shelter the homeless
5. Visit the sick
6. Visit those in prison
7. Bury the dead

STOP: Take a five minute flight with the Angel. You know what to do.

(Memory)   "Angel leading"
(Intellect)   "Help Tobit"
(Will)   "Be merciful"

Day 24 10.2 TOBIT IS HELPED
By the Angel Raphael: (Tobit 1–14)

Let us take a moment to recall that we are with the
Angels in the presence of God and pray: "Dear God,
I beg You to please give me the grace, to SPEAK to the
three powers of my soul, so my memory, my intellect,
and my will, will be for the greater Glory of God."

MEMORY: We see a holy man named Tobit. He is dressed in simple but tidy clothes. Tobit feared God and abstained from sin. He fed the hungry, gave clothes to the naked and was heroic in burying the dead. The Lord permitted Tobit to be made blind in order to test his patience like Job. He sent his son Tobit [Jr.] on a long journey to collect ten talents of silver which he lent.

The Lord sent the **Angel Raphael**, who appeared as a person, to accompany Tobit on the journey. We see the **Angel Raphael** and Tobit talking as they walk along the long journey. We see the **Angel Raphael** save Tobit from being devoured by a large fish. We hear the large splash. We hear the **Angel Raphael** advise Tobit to defeat the demon that was oppressing his new wife by praying and fasting. We see Tobit collecting the money. It was a very adventurous and successful trip.

When they returned home, the **Angel Raphael** cured Tobit Senior of his blindness. Tobit said,

"What can we give to this holy man (the Angel) for traveling with you?"

His son responded, "He traveled with me and brought me home safe again.

He received the money of Gabelus.
He caused me to have my wife.
He chased from her the evil spirit.
He gave joy to her parents.

Myself he delivered from being devoured by the fish. You also he has made to see the light of Heaven. We are filled with all good things through him" (Tobit 12:3).

For this Tobit and his son intended to give Raphael half the wealth they obtained. The **Angel Raphael** said, "Bless God of Heaven, give glory to Him, in the sight of all that live, because He has shown His mercy to you. Prayer is good with fasting and alms, more than to lay up treasures of gold. But they that commit sin and iniquity are enemies to their own soul . . . I am the **Angel Raphael**, one of the seven who stand before the throne of God. Peace be to you and fear not. When I was with you, it was by the will of God. Bless Him and sing praise to Him." Tobit and his family gave glory to God and prospered.

We are marveling about the way that the **Angel Raphael** healed Tobit's eyes.

INTELLECT: Why did God use Raphael to heal Tobit?

Remember, God does not always heal directly. Sometimes he uses men and Angels for instruments.

10.2 WILL: Some Angel members will be involved in healing ministries. Use the powerful and holy Name of Jesus and ask for Saint Raphael's help. After Jesus heals, always give thanks and glory to God.

STOP: Take a five minute flight with the Angel You know what to do.

(Memory)	"Angel Healing"
(Intellect)	"By God's Power"
(Will)	"Glory to God"

Day 25 11.1 THE ANGEL HELPS PHILIP
To Baptize: (Acts 8)

Let us take a moment to recall that we are with the Angels in the presence of God and pray: "Dear God, I beg You to please give me the grace, to SPEAK to the three powers of my soul, so my memory, my intellect, and my will, will be for the greater Glory of God."

MEMORY: We see the Deacon Philip baptize many people and make several miracles in Jesus's name. This prepared the people so that the bishops (apostles) Peter and John could lay their hands upon them in order to give the Sacrament of Confirmation. This enriched the people with the Holy Spirit (see Acts 8). We see the young man named Philip walking along the road. We see a beautiful Angel appear to him. We see Philip's face in awe; then he smiles. Now an Angel of the Lord spoke to Philip saying, "Arise, go towards the south" (Acts 8:26). Philip obeyed the Angel and found a chaste servant of the Queen (a eunuch) of great authority. The Spirit had Philip evangelize, explain the scriptures, and preach Jesus unto him.

We see the smile on the eunuch's face. We realize that he found the answer to the deepest longing of his heart. The eunuch was ready to embrace Jesus Christ. As they went their way, they came to a certain body of water and the eunuch said, "See, here is water. What hinders me from being baptized?" Philip replied, "If you believe with all your heart, you may." The eunuch answered, "I believe that Jesus Christ is the Son of God." So they went down into the water, both Philip and the eunuch, and he baptized him. We see the Eunuch kneel down in the shallow water and bow his head. We see Philip grab a shell and scoop out some water. We hear the splash of the water. We hear Philip say, "I baptize you in the name of the Father and of the Son and of the Holy Spirit." We see the large smile on the eunuch's face. And when they came out of the water, the Spirit of the Lord took away Philip; and the eunuch saw him no more, and he went his way rejoicing. We are impressed with how the Angel directed Philip to help the eunuch.

INTELLECT: How do we imitate the Angel? Baptism is a very important sacrament in building up the Kingdom of Christ. Philip used water. Jesus said, "Unless you are born again you cannot see the kingdom of God" (John 3:3). "How can a man be born again when he is old?" Jesus said, "Unless a man be born again of WATER and the HOLY SPIRIT, he cannot enter the Kingdom of God" (John 3:5). When a person is born the first time, he/she is a child of man. When he/she is born again by Baptism, he/she becomes a child of God. Baptism removes original sin caused by Adam and Eve through the power of the Redeemer, Jesus Christ. One must be a child of God before receiving Jesus in Holy Communion.

This is the true scriptural meaning to be born again. This interpretation of Baptism is confirmed by the Holy Spirit to the Church. Some people erroneously give a false meaning to born again and then discourage people from being baptized. John the Baptist testified to Baptism. Jesus and His apostles baptized with water and the Holy Spirit. With help from the Angels, Philip and the Church have been building up the Kingdom of God this way ever since. Jesus made it very clear, "Baptize them in the name of the Father, Son, and the Holy Spirit" (Matthew 28:19). Angel members will help with Baptism even if they are not the ones who do the actual Baptism.

11.1 WILL: Just as the Angel helped bring the eunuch together with Philip so he could be baptized, Angel members will help bringing together non-baptized people with the Lord's servants so that they may be baptized.

STOP: Take a five minute flight with the Angel. You know what to do.

(Memory)   "Water"
(Intellect)   "Children of God"
(Will)   "Help baptize"

Day 26 12.1–12.2 THE ANGEL HELPS
The Prophet Elijah:(1Kings 19)

Let us take a moment to recall that we are with the Angels in the presence of God and pray: "Dear God, I beg You to please give me the grace, to SPEAK to the three powers of my soul, so my memory, my intellect, and my will, will be for the greater Glory of God."

MEMORY: We see trees on the hills of Mount Carmel. We see a large number of people. We see a challenge and a victory. After Elijah defeated four hundred fifty false prophets of Baal (Devil) on Mount Carmel, Jezebel sent the army to have Elijah killed. Elijah fled into the desert. Elijah was tired, hungry, and told the Lord, "I can't take another step!" He asked the Lord that he might die. He slept under a juniper tree and behold, an **Angel of the Lord** touched him and said to him, "Arise and eat." He looked and there was by his head a hearth cake (bread), and a vessel of water. He ate and drank and fell asleep again. An Angel of the Lord came again the second time, touched him, and said to him, "Arise, eat for thou has yet a great way to go." And he arose, ate, and drank, and walked in the strength of that food for forty days and forty nights up to the mount of God, Horeb (see 1 Kings 19:5–8). After an earthquake, and a great fire, God appeared to Elijah in a gentle wind. Elijah exclaimed how the children of God have forsaken God's covenant. God used him to build up His Kingdom.

INTELLECT: How was Elijah strengthened in his journey?

The Angel strengthened Elijah with holy bread and water to continue his pilgrimage to the holy mountain of God. How do we imitate the Angel?

12.1 WILL: Angel members will encourage people to eat the true bread from Heaven (see John 6:52), Holy Communion, and drink from the Holy Spirit by means of prayer to Jesus and the other sacraments. This will strengthen them on their pilgrimage through the desert of this life to arrive at the true mountain of God, which is Heaven.

MEMORY: We see the Angel help the tired Elijah make a journey to the mountain.

INTELLECT: The Angel encouraged Elijah to climb the mountain of the Lord. How does that mountain relate to us today? The mountain of God is Heaven. Climbing it is the daily struggle to build up the virtues through the spiritual life that give glory to God.

The effect of Original Sin is that our souls are created good but we are inclined to evil (CCC #2903). If we do not put an effort to develop virtues, we are inclined to go downhill. We must, "climb the mountain of the Lord" (Isaiah 2:3–4).

Therefore, when we strive for union with God and building up the virtues of our soul that give us a capacity to love, that is what climbing the mountain of God means.

In the Psalm of David, Psalm 24 gives a challenge, "Who shall climb the mountain of the Lord, who shall stand in the Holy Place?" In Psalm 11, the question is asked, "How can you say to your soul, fly like a bird to its mountain." The answer is loving meditation or mental prayer will teach your soul how to fly. This will help others obtain and apply the grace received in Holy Communion and the other sacraments, in order to build up the Kingdom of God.

12.2 WILL: Angel members will help others with the spiritual life through meditation that will encourage and provide strength to develop the virtues, prepare the soul for Holy Communion and obtain grace to build up Christ's Kingdom on Earth and get to Heaven for eternity.

STOP: Take a five minute flight with the Angel.

You know what to do.

(Memory)	"Elijah's journey"
(Intellect)	"Given bread"
(Will)	"Promote Eucharist"

Day 27 12.3 THE ANGEL HELPS
The Prophet Elijah: (1Kings 19)

Let us take a moment to recall that we are with the Angels in the presence of God and pray: "Dear God, I beg You to please give me the grace, to SPEAK to the three powers of my soul, so my memory, my intellect, and my will, will be for the greater Glory of God."

MEMORY: We see trees on the hills of Mount Carmel.

We see a large number of people. We see a challenge and a victory. After Elijah defeated the four hundred fifty false prophets of Baal (Devil) on Mount Carmel, Jezebel sent the army to have Elijah killed. Elijah fled into the desert. Elijah was tired, hungry and asked the Lord that he might die. He slept under a juniper tree and behold, an **Angel of the Lord** touched him and said to him, "Arise and eat."

He looked and there was by his head a hearth cake (bread), and a vessel of water. He ate and drank and fell asleep again. An Angel of the Lord came again the second time, touched him, and said to him, "Arise, eat for thou has yet a great way to go." And he arose, ate, and drank, and walked in the strength of that food for forty days and forty nights up to the mount of God, Horeb (1 Kings 19:5–8). After an earthquake, and a great fire, God appeared to Elijah in a gentle wind. Elijah exclaimed how the children of God have forsaken God's covenant. God used Elijah to build up His Kingdom.

INTELLECT: Why did the Angel protect the prophet Elijah from the wicked Jezebel? How does the Angel's help to the prophet Elijah relate to us today? Just as the Angel encouraged Elijah THE PROPHET when Jezebel tried to kill him, Angel members will always help, encourage, and pray for the visionaries (prophets) of our days who God is using to re-establish His holy covenant (see Matthew 26:28).

The seers of formally approved apparition events such as Saint Catherine Laboure of Paris, Saint Bernadette of Lourdes, the children of Fatima, Kibeho (Rwanda), and the apparitions that have no official declarations, yet such as Medjugorje, Garabandal, Queen of Heaven and many others are always persecuted by the world. Angel members can learn, experience, and discern apparition events, but as section 4.4 makes clear, we will always humbly submit to the proper Church authorities.

Mental prayer will help Angel members with the discernment of spirits. False prophets lead people into sin. True prophets convert us away from sin and strengthen our love for God and our neighbor. In particular, they help us to renew God's holy covenant the way Elijah did.

(First John 4: 2-3) helps to guide us in the discernment of spirits. "By this, the Spirit of God is known. Every spirit which confesses that Jesus Christ is come in the flesh (The Incarnation and the Holy Communion) is of God. And every spirit that denies Jesus is not of God.

This is the Antichrist of whom you have heard. He is now already in the world."

The Antichrist will always try to take the hidden Jesus (Eucharist) away from us.

12.3 The Angel members will protect and encourage the prophets of God when they are attacked.

STOP: Take a five minute flight with the Angel. You know what to do.

(Memory)   "Evil attacks"

(Intellect)   "Battle"

(Will)   "Defend true prophets"

Day 28 13.1-13.2 JESUS WITH THE ANGELS
At the Last Judgment: (Matthew 25:31–46)

Let us take a moment to recall that we are with the Angels in the presence of God and pray: "Dear God, I beg You to please give me the grace, to SPEAK to the three powers of my soul, so my memory, my intellect, and my will, will be for the greater Glory of God."

MEMORY: We see Jesus. He appears in bright white clothes. He looks peaceful but powerful. We see a multitude of Angels around His feet, worshipping Him. We hear Jesus say, "And when the Son of Man shall come in His Majesty, and all the **Angels** with Him, then shall He sit upon the seat of His Majesty and all the nations shall be gathered together before Him, and He shall separate them one from the other as the shepherd separates sheep from the goats. And He shall set the sheep on His right hand, but the goats on His left."

"Then shall the king say to those on His right hand: 'Come, you blessed of My Father, possess the kingdom prepared for you from the foundation of the world. For I was hungry, and you gave Me to eat; I was thirsty, and you gave Me to drink; I was a stranger, and you took Me in: Naked and you clothed Me: sick and you visited Me: I was in prison and you came to Me.'"

"Then shall the just answer Him, saying: 'Lord, when did we see You hungry, and feed You; thirsty, and give You a drink? When did we see You a stranger, and take You in? Or naked and clothe You? Or when did we see You sick or in prison and visit You?' And the king answered: 'Amen I say to you, as long as you did it to one of these least of My brothers, you did it to Me.'

"Then He shall say to them also that shall be on His left hand: 'Depart from Me you cursed, into everlasting fire which was prepared for the Devil and his Angels. For I was hungry and you gave Me nothing to eat. I was thirsty and you gave Me no drink. I was a stranger, and you took Me not in: Naked and you did not cloth Me: sick and in prison, and you did not visit Me.'

"Then they shall also answer Him saying: 'Lord when did we see Thee hungry, or thirsty, or a stranger, or naked, or sick, or in prison, and did not minister to You?' Then He shall answer them, saying: 'Amen I say to you, as long as you did it not to the least of these, neither did you do it to Me. And these shall go into ever lasting punishment: but the just into life everlasting'" (Matthew 25:31–46). We see the look of hope and horror on the Angel's faces as Jesus describes everlasting punishment or eternal life.

INTELLECT: Where are they going forever? Either we are going to spend all of eternity extremely happy in Heaven or extremely miserable in the fires of Hell. How do we end up with the good Angels at the judgment?
How can I choose Heaven?

13.1 WILL: Mental prayer will help you choose wisely and obtain the grace to live wisely. Our priority will be to live with our souls in the state of grace and give glory to God. Our will is going to direct our pilgrimages in life and determine how much eternal reward to enjoy or how much eternal punishment to endure.

MEMORY: We see Jesus separating the sheep from the goats. We see the look of hope and horror on the Angel's faces as Jesus describes everlasting punishment or eternal life.

INTELLECT: How did Jesus decide who to separate? Jesus used the deeds of mercy as a primary basis for Judgment. Jesus made it clear to love God and to love our neighbor, especially the least of our brothers.

13.2 WILL: Therefore, remember the A, B, C's of mercy:

<u>A</u>sk for His mercy! <u>B</u>e merciful! <u>C</u>omplete trust! Practicing this mercy is an effective way to keep your soul humble and on the right track.

STOP: Take a five minute flight with the Angel. You know what to do.

(Memory)	"Horrors of Hell"
(Intellect)	"Judgment Criteria"
(Will)	"Be Merciful"

Day 29 13.3 JESUS WITH THE ANGELS
At the Last Judgment: (Matthew 25: 31–46)

Let us take a moment to recall that we are with the Angels in the presence of God and pray: "Dear God, I beg You to please give me the grace, to SPEAK to the three powers of my soul, so my memory, my intellect, and my will, will be for the greater Glory of God."

MEMORY: We see Jesus. He appears in bright white clothes. He looks peaceful, but powerful. We see a multitude of Angels around His feet, worshipping Him. We hear Jesus say, "And when the Son of Man shall come in His Majesty, and all the **Angels** with Him, then shall He sit upon the seat of His Majesty and all the nations shall be gathered together before Him, and He shall separate them one from the other as the shepherd separates sheep from the goats. And He shall set the sheep on His right hand, but the goats on His left."

"Then shall the king say to those on His right hand: 'Come, you blessed of My Father, possess the kingdom prepared for you from the foundation of the world. For I was hungry, and you gave Me to eat; I was thirsty, and you gave Me to drink; I was a stranger, and you took Me in: Naked and you clothed Me: sick and you visited Me: I was in prison and you came to Me.'"

"Then shall the just answer Him, saying: 'Lord, when did we see You hungry, and feed You; thirsty, and give You a drink? When did we see You a stranger, and take You in? Or naked and clothe You? Or when did we see You sick or in prison and visit You?' And the king answered: 'Amen I say to you, as long as you did it to one of these least of My brothers, you did it to Me.' "Then He shall say to them also that shall be on His left hand: 'Depart from Me you cursed, into everlasting fire which was prepared for the Devil and his Angels. For I was hungry and you gave Me nothing to eat. I was thirsty and you gave Me no drink. I was a stranger, and you took Me not in: Naked and you did not cloth Me: sick and in prison, and you did not visit Me.'

"Then they shall also answer Him saying: 'Lord when did we see Thee hungry, or thirsty, or a stranger, or naked, or sick, or in prison, and did not minister to You?' Then He shall answer them, saying: 'Amen I say to you, as long as you did it not to the least of these, neither did you do it to Me. And these shall go into everlasting punishment: but the just into life everlasting'" (Matth.25:31–46).

We see the look of hope and horror on the Angel's faces as Jesus describes everlasting punishment or eternal life. We hear Jesus say, "Whatever you did not do to the least of My brothers, you did not do it to Me."

INTELLECT: Why are the deeds of mercy so important? Jesus challenges us in the Gospel not only to live the Ten Commandments, but to love God and our fellow man.

Not only "Thou shalt not kill," but "Whatever you did not do for the least of My brothers, you did not do for Me." This sheds light on the terrible sin of abortion. The least of our brothers are murdered every day. In America since January 1973, one child has been murdered in the womb for every two children born alive. This will prove to future generations that our society is in the Devil's grip. Go to the encyclopedia and look up embryology. Look at the pictures of the baby in the mother's womb. Mental prayer will help you see through the fancy expressions of *first trimester*. Show a seven-year-old child a picture of a child in the twelfth week of development, and the child will tell you it is a little baby. Note that twelve weeks is within the time period of the first trimester.

In 1981, the United States Senate Bill 158 entitled the Human Life Bill, petitioned scientists about their knowledge of the facts of human life. In an overwhelming agreement, they declared that it is a scientific fact that human life begins upon conception. A unique individual is alive and even the color of his or her eyes is already determined. The Holy Catholic Church believes that abortion is murder except when the doctors are directly saving the life of a mother but indirectly aborting the child.

The Bible clearly teaches that when Mary visited Her cousin Elizabeth, the **baby** in Elizabeth's womb leapt for joy (Luke 1:41–5). Also, Elizabeth, filled with the Holy Spirit called Mary the "Theotokos" or "Mother of God." In other words, she confirmed that Jesus was in Mary's womb. When you attack the least of my brothers, you attack Jesus. Remember, Jesus forgives, Jesus forgives, Jesus forgives, but we must repent and not persist in our errors.

The Devil demands human sacrifice and it gives him much power over our society. This is a supernatural battle. At Fatima, Our Lady did not call for an army of preachers, but of people who pray and fast. She knows what we need is an evangelization that is closer to an exorcism than reasonable persuasion.

God sent Our Lady to give us a simple yet powerful solution to fighting the evils of our society today, especially abortion. That solution is praying the daily Rosary along with the Fatima Five First Saturdays or Communion of Reparation Devotion. We are all called to help. The Five First Saturday Devotion uses the supernatural powers that come from Jesus Christ through the One, Holy, Catholic, and Apostolic Church. This is the only solution that will be successful. It is a solution that gives glory to God. It is a solution that will convert us back to God.

The Fatima devotion consist of the following:

For five consecutive first Saturdays of the month:

1. Pray five decades of the Rosary.

2. Go to Mass and receive Holy Communion.

3. Go to Confession (within eight days before or after).

4. Meditate (Mental Prayer) for fifteen minutes on the fifteen (now twenty) mysteries of the Rosary.
5. Offer all this up for the sins and blasphemies against the Immaculate Heart of Mary.

God's promises to those who practice this devotion are very powerful. Not only will Russia be converted, but, to those who practice this, God will send Our Lady at the hour of death with enough graces for salvation.

13.3 WILL: Angel members will evangelize the daily Rosary and the Fatima Five First Saturday Devotion to fight abortion and promote conversion. Angel members will also carefully review the three secrets of Fatima as revealed by the Church (see the Vatican web site www. vatican.va).

STOP: Take a five minute flight with the Angel. You know what to do.

(Memory)	"Sheep – goats"
(Intellect)	"Heaven – Hell"
(Will)	"First Saturdays"

Day 30 14.1 THE ANGEL GUIDES
SAINT JOSEPH (Matthew 2:13–21)

Let us take a moment to recall that we are with the Angels in the presence of God and pray: "Dear God, I beg You to please give me the grace, to SPEAK to the three powers of my soul, so my memory, my intellect, and my will, will be for the greater Glory of God."

MEMORY: We see St. Joseph. He is sleeping. There is a peaceful look on his face. The expression on his face changes. Behold, an **Angel of the Lord** appeared to Joseph in his sleep and said, "Arise, and take the Child and His mother, and flee into Egypt: and stay there until I shall tell you. For it will come to pass that Herod will seek the Child to destroy Him" (Matthew 2:13). Then Herod, perceiving he was deluded by the wise men, was exceedingly angry; and sending (soldiers) killed all the men children in Bethlehem . . . from two years old and younger (Matthew 2:16).

INTELLECT: How did the Angel's message influence them? The Angel protected the Holy Family. With the divorce rate in America over fifty percent, everyone is realizing that families are under attack; however, they are not sure what to do about it. It is a spiritual attack.

14.1 WILL: Angel members will evangelize the Holy Rosary as a remedy for attacks against families. The Rosary will help because:

A. Prayer provides a union with God who is the source of True Love.

B. The Rosary is the Weapon against the Devil (see section 2.5).

C. During the joyful mysteries, we meditate upon the Holy Family. Everyone will learn from their example. Joseph gives us a model of watchfulness and care. Mary gives us an ideal model of love, modesty, submission and perfect loyalty. Children have Jesus' obedience to admire and copy. Watching Joseph, Mary and Jesus will sweeten the burdens in this life and protect the families (Pope Leo XIII).

STOP: Take a five minute flight with the Angel. You know what to do.

(Memory)   "Families attacked"

(Intellect)   "Protection"

(Will)   "Pray Rosary"

Day 31 14.2–14.3 THE ANGEL GUIDES SAINT JOSEPH (Matthew 2:13–21)

Let us take a moment to recall that we are with the Angels in the presence of God and pray: "Dear God, I beg You to please give me the grace, to SPEAK to the three powers of my soul, so my memory, my intellect, and my will, will be for the greater Glory of God."

MEMORY: We see St. Joseph. He is sleeping. There is a peaceful look on his face. The expression on his face changes. Behold, an **Angel of the Lord** appeared to Joseph in his sleep and said, "Arise, and take the Child and His mother, and flee into Egypt: and stay there until I shall tell you. For it will come to pass that Herod will seek the Child to destroy Him" (Matthew 2:13). Then Herod, perceiving he was deluded by the wise men, was exceedingly angry; and sending (soldiers) killed all the men children in Bethlehem . . . from two years old and younger (Matthew 2:16).
We are attracted to the way the Angel is speaking to St. Joseph.

INTELLECT: How does the Angel's message apply to the future? The Angel told the Holy Family to flee into exile to escape death. Similarly, Jesus told us that before His Kingship takes place the Antichrist, the Son of Perdition, or the Devil in the form of a man will appear claiming to be Christ. Angel members will recognize him because the

Devil was a murderer from the beginning. The Antichrist will promote the Culture of Death. This will be a time when our Angels will guide us to safety. Remember always, Jesus gave us the Gospel of Life and Jesus came that we might have life and have it more abundantly (see John 10:10). See the encyclical, *Evangelium Vitae*, by Pope John Paul II (March 25, 1995).

Actually, the religion of the Beast is the Anti-Gospel of Life or the Culture of Death. This will be the eventual full flowering of the "Dictatorship of moral relativism" (see Pope Benedict XVI's "Light of the World" Chapter 5). In the name of tolerance, they are totally intolerant. Eventually if one does not belong to that religion, they will prevent you from buying or selling (see Revelation 13:14–18). Their religion is abortion, contraception, euthanasia, anti-marriage, anti-Christian practices on demand.

The Antichrist will try to get us to break our Covenant with God. In other words, he will try to trick us into not receiving the fruit from the Tree of Life or the Eucharist / Holy Communion.

14.2 WILL: Angel members will not follow leaders who promote the Culture of Death or break our covenant with God. They will follow Jesus Christ and the Gospel of Life.

MEMORY: Behold an **Angel of the Lord** appeared in sleep to Joseph in Egypt saying, "Arise, and take the Child and His mother, and go to the land of Israel. For they are dead who sought the life of the Child" (Matthew 2:20).

INTELLECT: Why is the Angel telling them to return?
Remember that even in exile Jesus and Mary will always be with us, and that exile will be temporary.

14.3 WILL: In all difficult situations, Angel members will have hope that someday things will improve. We will remain thankful that Jesus, Mary and the Angels are always with us.

STOP: Take a five minute flight with the Angel. You know what to do.

(Memory)   "Families attacked"
(Intellect)   "Diabolic battle"
(Will)   "Faithful to Jesus"

Day 32 15.1 ANGELS AT JESUS' ASCENSION into Heaven: (Acts 1: 10–12)

Let us take a moment to recall that we are with the Angels in the presence of God and pray: "Dear God, I beg You to please give me the grace, to SPEAK to the three powers of my soul, so my memory, my intellect, and my will, will be for the greater Glory of God."

MEMORY: We see Jesus dressed in white. He is smiling. We hear the apostles ask Jesus, "Lord, will you at this time restore again the kingdom to Israel?" (see Acts 1:6–11)

"A cloud received Jesus out of their sight. **Two men [Angels] stood by dressed in white** and said, "Men of Galilee, why do you look up in the sky? This Jesus who you see going to Heaven will come again the same way as you seen Him going to Heaven."

INTELLECT: How will Jesus return? Jesus will return on a cloud. How does Jesus's coming again make us feel? It brings us a sense of hope and motivation to carry out His commands.

15.1 WILL: Angel members will always deliver this same message of hope. Jesus Christ will return on a cloud for all to see; and we are praying for this (see Luke 21:27). Note: The false Christ will not return miraculously on a cloud.

MEMORY: We see the Angel speaking to the disciples as they are looking up into the clouds.

INTELLECT: Why are not more people preparing for His coming?

Many people did not recognize the baby Jesus because they mistakenly thought the Messiah would be an earthly king. The Kingdom of Jesus will reign in our hearts and in Heaven. True love is the key to the reign. The false, earthly Messiah will probably enter into the Golden Gate of Jerusalem. Those not accepting that Jesus Christ, the Son of God already fulfilled that prophecy will probably follow the false Christ.

15.2 WILL: Angel members will prepare by having Jesus Reign in our hearts. They will consecrate themselves to the Sacred Hearts of Jesus and the Immaculate Heart of Mary to prepare for that Reign. Mental prayer is the key to His Reign.

MEMORY: Jesus Christ's last words before the Ascension were, "Go, preach the Gospel to every creature . . . and know I am with you always, even to the end of the world."

INTELLECT: Jesus Christ is King of the Angels. He will be with us on our mission while learning how to meditate and teaching others how to meditate.

15.3 WILL: Start your journey with some examples of meditation. Evangelize by sharing the fruit of your meditations. Do not be afraid to share the fruit of your meditations. Always remember your vow to God and the Angels to promise to beg Him for the grace that the three powers of your soul —the memory, the intellect, and the will—will be for the greater glory of God. Amen.

STOP: Take a five minute flight with the Angel. You know what to do.

(Memory)   "Jesus and Clouds"

(Intellect)   "Hope"

(Will)   "Share meditations"

Day 33

SAMPLE MEDITATION:

The Blessed Virgin Mary appeared to Saint Ignatius of Loyola and dictated to him the Spiritual Exercises in which we learn how to meditate. Angel members are encouraged to go on retreats and to meditate. A spiritual retreat is an internal adventure with God. God can launch your soul like a rocket. You may not know where God will take you, but be bold, be brave, and trust in Him as your soul flies with the Angels.

Meditation engages thought, imagination, emotion, and desire (#2708 Catechism). A brief summary of meditation will help Angel members get familiar with the steps involved. This is only a brief summary. The more complete steps can be done on a retreat.

When people try to meditate, sometimes their minds draw a blank. These steps along with the fifteen stories of Angels in the Bible will help to foster the meditation experience.

SEVEN STEPS OF MEDITATION

The seven steps to meditation can be compared to the steps in driving a car.

At first, these steps may seem difficult. There are so many details to worry about. After some practice, they both become easy and fun.

As your soul spends time watching Jesus and Mary in <u>their</u> lives, you will grow spiritually and be able to see Jesus and Mary at work in <u>your</u> life. This is how to achieve mental prayer's ultimate goal of living life with the living God. In other words, meditation leads to the highest form of prayer, which is contemplation. Before you learn how to walk you must crawl. Before you learn how to fly you must learn how to drive.

STEP ONE: SELECT CAR'S DESTINATION.
Select a meditation. (The First Christmas)

STEP TWO: GET IN THE CAR.
Get in the frame of meditation by recalling that you are with the Angels in the presents of God. (God is everywhere)

STEP THREE: START THE ENGINE.
Start the meditation by praying. Dear God, I beg You, to please give me the grace that the three powers of my soul, my memory, my intellect, and my will, will be for the greater glory of God.

STEP FOUR: PUT THE GEAR IN DRIVE.
Memory: To move forward on the meditation, use the power of your soul, the memory. Ask the question "What". What do I see? What do I hear? What do I feel? What do I smell?

STEP FIVE: TURN THE STEERING WHEEL.
Intellect: Use the power of your soul, the intellect to direct your meditation by asking the question "Why". During the memory, the Holy Spirit may start speaking to you by attracting your attention to something. It is usually a clear image that is in your mind, then you ask "Why" to start analyzing the subject. Since knowledge and wisdom are gifts from the Holy Spirit, sometimes God gives you the answer right away. Other times, He has you ponder and ask Why for a very long time before He enlightens your intellect with the answer.

STEP SIX: PRESS ON THE GAS PEDAL.
Will: Use the power of the soul, the Will to make a RESOLUTION in your life based on the meditation. "I will try . . ." If you do not use the gas pedal, you do not really go anywhere. If you do not use the will in a meditation, it does not help your soul too much.

STEP SEVEN: Colloquy
After enjoying the trip, come back home and park the car. Conclude the meditation by thanking God. (Colloquy) Dear God, I thank You for giving me the grace, that the three powers of my soul, my memory, my intellect, and my will, will be for the greater glory of God.

EXAMPLE 1 - STEP 1: **PRELUDE. Choose the subject of "Christmas" for meditation. Saint Ignatius recommended we meditate for one hour on a subject. The Holy Spirit will guide you.**

STEP 2: This step should be short and a preparation for meditation, compared to getting in the car. It consists of asking Jesus for something and making a picture in your mind about the subject. For example, look at the statues in the Christmas scene and recall that you are with the Angels in the presence of God. Also, ask Him for a specific gift: "Help me to be more wise and courageous."

STEP 3: Start the Car. Say, "Dear God, I beg You to please give me the grace that the three powers of my soul, my memory, my intellect, and my will, will be for the greater glory of God."
BODY–Consists of three parts: the memory, the intellect, and the will.

STEP 4: The Memory, in which we recall the subject and ask questions such as WHAT—**What do I see? What do I hear? What do I feel? What do I smell?** I see Mary dressed in blue and white and Joseph dressed in red and white. They are smiling. Jesus is wrapped in white swaddling clothes and laying in a manger. We see an ox, donkey, and a multitude of the Heavenly Angels around. We hear the Angels saying, "Holy, holy,

holy." We hear the animals. We smell the aroma of a barn. We feel the cold of the night air, but joy is still bursting from Mary and Joseph's eyes as they look at the Baby Jesus.

STEP 5: The Intellect, in which we reflect and analyze the subject. Ask questions of WHY—Why are there so many Angels? It must be a very important event. They are cold and IN poverty. A comfortable house is not making them happy. Why are Mary and Joseph so joyful? They must love Baby Jesus very much. When they have Jesus, they have everything to make them happy. Why are they in a stable? Because they are poor and there is no room for them in the inn. Why was Jesus born poor? To prove to us that God loves the poor.

STEP 6: The Will, in which we make a resolution regarding the subject. Make the statement, "I WILL TRY . . ." I will try to love Jesus more than I love my earthly attachments. Only through this proper order of affection in my soul, will I experience peace and obtain happiness.

STEP 7: COLLOQUY. Sweet conversation with Jesus as a friend. Jesus, thank You for coming to us on Christmas day. Thank You for teaching us, not only by word, but by example. Thank You for making it so easy to love You.

Dear God, I thank You for giving me the grace that the three powers of my soul—my memory, my intellect, and my will—will always be for the greater glory of God. Amen.

Of course, since the Holy Spirit's knowledge is infinite, God can inspire us with a multitude of questions, insights and resolutions for each meditation. Even if it is the same subject, new fruit will be obtained. In the *Spiritual Exercises,* Saint Ignatius writes points and insights that help with the meditations.

> Congratulations Angel member!
> You made the thirty-three days!
> Your soul is now ready to fly.
> Have fun and give glory to God.

"What happens when I finish the Angel Constitution?" Ben asked.

The Angel replied, "Many things, for one, you will achieve the Seraphim level of Angel membership. You will also be prepared to go on a St. Ignatius retreat, not only for a weekend, but also even up to 30 days. In addition to this, there are other spiritual exercises that the Angel Constitution will teach you. You will become a master of mental prayer."

II.1 The Angel of the New Era Beginnings

Encountering God by using the three powers of the soul is within the grasp of every human being. This type of encounter is called mental prayer. After taking a novena of trips (nine times) to Medjugorje, Father Francis Budovic, S.J., felt inspired to begin a lay apostolate to encourage mental prayer. Every creature of God has a purpose or mission in life. Mental prayer will help souls understand their purpose and obtain strength to fulfill their mission. Even souls who know their mission in life, or have an apostolate, will benefit by mental prayer. The true Spirit of Vatican II calls for Lay People to become more active in evangelizing the secular world— to be the salt of the Earth (Lumen Gentium chapter IV, 33). The Angels of the New Era can be the "salt" for all apostolates because mental prayer is vital for members to be an effective instrument of the Holy Spirit.

The first official Angels of the New Era retreat was held in January 1996, in the suburbs of Chicago. Father Francis suggested a Constitution for the lay apostolate as the number of Angel members increased. Fr. Francis commissioned an Angel Member, who was on several pilgrimages with Fr. Francis, to write the Constitution. This Angel member, who is a third order Dominican, felt inspired during a pilgrimage to Medjugorje to write this Constitution, based on Father Francis's teaching of mental prayer.

At a pilgrimage during Easter of 1998, the Angel member was walking across the fields in Medjugorje. A great tiredness overtook him, so he went off the path and took a nap in the field. The last thing he remembered was looking at the length of the leash of a cow, to ensure he would not get stepped on while sleeping. When he awoke, he sensed the presence of Our Lady and the Angels and the Constitution was in his head. On August 18, 2020 he was able to give the Constitution to Pope John Paul II and asked him to bless the Lay Apostolate that would help young people to meditate. Pope John Paull II made the sign of the cross on his forehead and he felt his knees buckle and almost fell down through the holy blessing that he is sure will be transferred to all Angel members. The word "Speak" was added to the vow on October 22, 2020 (Feast of St. John Paul II) during the retreat of Spiritual Exercises at Garabandal, Spain. Father Francis is a Jesuit priest (Society of Jesus). The founder of the Jesuit order is Saint Ignatius of Loyola. Saint Ignatius wrote the *Spiritual Exercises.* Our Lady and the Child Jesus appeared to St. Ignatius in a cave at Manresa, Spain and dictated the *Spiritual Exercises* to him. Religious orders and diocesan priests from all over the world use the *Spiritual Exercises* for retreats. It helps them grow in mental prayer, which strengthens and supports their ministry to serve Jesus Christ.

At the beginning, there was an obstacle to the formation of the Angel Constitution. The Jesuits and the Dominicans had an age-old difficulty: "Is it the individual's will or God's grace that is everything when it comes to building up our treasure in Heaven?" After visiting Medjugorje, we came to the conclusion: "By the grace of God He gave us a free will. Man must use his free will to embrace the grace." This compromise was satisfactory, and the Angel constitution moved forward.

The Angel of the New Era will be an apostolate for the New Millennium. It is not meant to replace other apostolates, but rather to strengthen them.

Saint John Paul II the Great said, "to contemplate the face of Christ at the school of Mary is the program that I am setting up for the Church in the new millennium" (Encyclical Letter on The Eucharist). Angel members of this lay apostolate will receive instruction and grace in learning how to meditate, so they can teach others how to meditate. Mental prayer will greatly strengthen and support these lay people in however they choose to serve Jesus Christ, the King of Kings.

II.2 ANGEL MEMBERSHIP AND THE VOW:

To become an Angel Member, one must take the Angel Vow. The vow is to promise to often *recall that we are with the Angels in the presence of God and pray: "Dear God, I beg You to please give me the grace, to speak to the three powers of my soul, so my memory, my intellect, and my will, will be for the greater Glory of God."*

The primary focus of Angel members will be to renew the vow of the apostolate often. In God's time the Holy Spirit will place a burning desire into your soul to read the fifteen Scripture passages of Angels in order to live out the Angel member's mission.

NOTE: This burning desire will occur at different times for different people. Therefore, focus on renewing the vow and God will let you know when the time is right for you.

Remember, "Ask and you will receive, seek and you will find, knock and it shall be open to you" (Matthew 7:7). God wants to give us graces, but He also wants His children to ask for these Good Things. As Angel members beg Him for these graces, He, in His infinite Love, will be happy to shower them down upon us. God's grace will sprout up saints upon the earth the same way the rain causes flowers to sprout up in springtime.

II.3 RENEWAL OF THE VOW

The vow is to be renewed often—every day if possible.

If something makes an Angel member think of an Angel, then say the prayer, "Dear God, I beg You to please give me the grace to speak to the three powers of my soul—so my memory, my intellect, and my will—will be for the greater glory of God." This grace that God will give us is very important to our souls. Remember, the soul is the part of us that lives forever. Our souls will live forever happy with God in Heaven or forever tortured with Satan in the fires of Hell. We choose, with the power of our will, a lifestyle on Earth that dictates our future reward. Angel members recommend that new members write their vow on a picture of an Angel Scene, and sign and date it. Place the picture in a location that will make it easy for you to repeat the vow often.

In order to become masters of mental prayer, we must also build up our souls with spiritual exercises, particularly daily prayer (especially Mass and the Holy Rosary) and Saint Ignatius of Loyola's *Spiritual Exercises*. Good counsel would advise to start slowly with the daily Peace Rosary. This consists of the Apostles Creed and seven Our Fathers, Hail Marys, and Glory Be prayers. A spiritual exercise is something by which we exercise or build up the three powers of the soul. If we are faithful to the vow, we will receive many graces.

Mental prayer will make faith come alive to us. Angel members will say, like the two disciples who met Jesus on the road to Emmaus: "Was not our heart burning within us, while (Jesus) spoke and opened to us the scriptures?" (Luke 24:32). This burning desire will help us to live the Constitution. Angel members will not only do spiritual exercises; this burning desire will have their souls Training for the Olympics of spirituality.

II.4 What is meant by "Angels"?

The word "Angel" means messenger servant of God. Angels are messengers by their function, not by their nature. By nature, Angels are pure spirits. Similarly, we are Angels by function, not by nature. By nature, we have a body and a soul.

The Bible states that we are created as less than the Angels (Psalms 8:6, Hebrews 2:7). However, Jesus gave us opportunities on Earth to build up our treasure in Heaven (see Matthew 6:20). The Devil tries to trick us into foolishly breaking our covenant with God, thus giving away our Heavenly inheritance and spending all of eternity as slaves to him. Mental prayer will help us to make wise decisions in regard to things on Earth and in Heaven.

The new *Catechism of the Catholic Church* states that "Christ is the center of the Angelic world. They are His Angels" (#331) and "The whole life of the Church benefits from the mysterious and powerful help of Angels" (#334). For the most part, Angels are invisible because they are pure spirits. Angel members will strive for profound humility so their work will become visible only when God wills it. Angel members will pray for humility and purity. Obtaining these virtues will always be the biggest battle mankind faces. Pray not only for purity in body, but for purity in your intentions as well. Ulterior motives give the Devil more opportunities to interfere with your missions.

NOTE: For Angel members who belong to the Church, the mystical Body of Christ, there are two things we can do on Earth as adopted sons of God, which the Angels cannot do in Heaven.
1. We can receive Holy Communion in our bodies.
2. We can offer up sacrifices to God and our sufferings in union with Jesus Christ to the Father.
Therefore, Angel members will both listen to and imitate the Angels in Heaven and focus on these two important things to best help bring about Jesus's Kingship on Earth as it is in Heaven. This will help us to be an imitation of Jesus Christ or to become saints.

II.5 What is meant by "Last Days/ New Era"?
Peter, our first pope describes the "Last Days/ New Era". After the Ascension of the Lord, they were

persevering with one mind in prayer with the women, and with Mary the Mother of Jesus and with His brethren (see Acts 1:14).

On Pentecost Sunday, there came a sound from Heaven, as of a mighty wind coming, and it filled the whole house where they were sitting. There appeared to them parted tongues as it were of fire, and it sat upon every one of them. They were all filled with the Holy Spirit and began to speak (see Acts 2:2–4).

Peter, standing up, said, "It shall come to pass, in the **Last Days**, says the Lord, I will pour out of my spirit upon all flesh: and your sons and your daughters shall prophesy, and your young men shall see visions and your old men shall dream dreams . . . and I will show wonders in the Heavens above and signs on the earth beneath" (Acts 2:17–19).

So, the Last Days/ New Era are those in which the Holy Spirit will use his messenger servants (Angels) to renew the face of the earth. As the remainder of Acts shows, God will help this renewal by some powerful wake up calls (see Acts 2:19–21).

Since the earth will be renewed, the Last Days are also the New Era.

At first, the apostles were too afraid to evangelize. Once the Holy Spirit came upon them, they were very bold and very effective.

II.6 THE ANGEL MEMBER'S MISSION

The primary mission of the Angels of the New Era is to learn how to meditate and then to teach others how to meditate. This will be the means for helping to spread Jesus's Kingship on Earth.

To meditate means to use the three powers of the soul to ponder a truth more deeply.

Mental Prayer means to use the three powers of the soul to encounter God.

The ultimate purpose of Mental Prayer is to begin living life with the living God.

Angel members will watch and imitate the good Angels while learning how to meditate.

In order to be a messenger, one has to listen to the message. Meditation is the key to learning how to listen to the Holy Spirit: "Speak Lord your servant is listening" (1 Samuel 3:10).

The keys to mental prayer are the gifts given to you by God, the Holy Spirit. God speaks to the sould through these gifts. They can come as thoughts or images to the mind or heart. Remember the gifts of the Holy Spirit include Wisdom, Knowledge, and Understanding (see Isaiah 11:2–3).

In order to renew the face of the earth, these gifts must bear fruit in our souls; particularly, the twelve fruits of the Holy Spirit, which include love, joy, peace, patience, kindness, faith, and chastity.

In Revelation 2 and 3, Jesus writes messages to the Angels during the Last Days: "He that has an ear, let

him hear what the Spirit says to the churches"
(Revelation 3:22). Since the members of Angels of
the New Era have ears, we will continue to pray,
"Speak, Lord, Your servants are listening."

II.7 WHY MEDITATE?

The five reasons why the Angel members will
meditate include:

1. To live life with the living God as we build up His
   Kingdom.
2. To build up treasure in Heaven.
3. To avoid the snares of the Devil.
4. To receive consolation from the Holy Spirit.
5. To love God with all our hearts, minds, souls, and
   bodies.

In doing so, the Holy Spirit will renew the face of
the earth, save other souls from the fires of Hell and
bring about Jesus's Kingship.

II.8 THE LORD'S KINGSHIP

The Angels in Heaven help serve the throne of God.
Someday, Jesus Christ will reign as King of our
hearts on Earth as He reigns in Heaven. Jesus said,
"Seek ye first the Kingdom of God" (Matth. 6:33).
The members of the lay apostolate of Angels of the
New Era will help to bring about this reign.
Members will help by becoming instruments of the
Holy Spirit.

Biblical Angel Stories: There are many stories of Angels helping out in the Bible from which we can draw insights. There are FIFTEEN specific stories of Angels in the Bible that describe the **MISSION OF** Angels of the New Era.

The Great Battle: The great battle of our day comes from worldwide international forces led by the prince of this world to get the three powers of the soul, the memory, the intellect, and the will, to rebel against God. This is a spiritual battle.

II.9 ANGEL MEMBERSHIP

Each member's name will be put on the Angels' list and a Holy Mass will be offered up for all Angel members on the thirteenth day of each month. Angel members can register their names at an authorized Angel of the Last Day center or on the Internet. This list will be taken around the world to various holy pilgrimage shrines in order to petition Heaven to bestow graces on all members. Father Francis Budovic delegated to Guy Murphy who will authorize these centers or will delegate another Angel member/s to accomplish this task. If possible/available, Angel members will also receive an Angel medal blessed by the Pope (General Audience) and allegedly by Our Lady of Medjugorje. This medal is a sacramental that God can use to pour out graces upon the members. It will also remind us that we have a guardian Angel and to pray for Saint Michael's intercession.

II.10 WHO CAN JOIN?

Anyone who is willing to take the vow can join the Angels of the New Era. There are lay Catholics, priests, sisters, non-Catholics, and even those unbaptized who are Angel members. There are no dues or fees associated with membership. Members can participate only to the degree that they are allowed to by the Church, and their churches. We have great confidence that even the unbaptized will receive so much grace that in the Lord's time they will not only convert to the Church that Jesus Christ established, but also be leaders with great humility, boldness, enthusiasm, and love. We invite you to adopt a missionary priest and give him a stipend to offer up Mass for Angel Members.

II.11 SPIRITUAL GROWTH

Angel members are encouraged to grow spiritually, "build up your treasure in Heaven." They can advance in the choir. There are nine choirs of Angels. Advancements are not recorded on paper. It is only known between the Angel member and God. Those who take the Angel Vow can submit their name in order to get more graces available to them.

CHOIR DESCRIPTION

Angel Member: Take the Angel Vow (Sec II.2).

Seraphim: Read/Pray the entire Angel Constitution. (In a thirty-three-day period)

Cherubim: Go on a retreat or pilgrimage.

Thrones: Evangelize one person to take the vow.

Dominions: Evangelize ten persons to take the vow.

Powers: Consecrate yourself to Jesus through Mary (Sec 6.9).

Virtues: Have your soul in the state of grace (see John 20:22-23).

Principalities: Examine your conscience daily.

Archangel: Frequently pray the Rosary as a weapon against evil.

Angel: Adore Jesus in the Blessed Sacrament.

Sons and Daughters of God: Renew God's covenant by receiving Jesus with love in Holy Communion.

III. PATRON SAINTS-ANGELS/ NEW ERA

Angel members will be part of the spiritual army that the Holy Spirit will use to help bring Jesus Christ's Kingship to renew the face of the earth. As told by the Scriptures, the Heavenly court will be joining the battle. The Blessed Virgin Mary is Queen of the Angels and our Queen. The scriptures testify that She meditated often on the life of Christ by "pondering these things in her heart . . ." (Luke 2:19). She, along with **St. Joseph**, will be the primary intercessor for Angels of the New Era in order to best help bring about Jesus's Kingdom upon Earth. It was Our Lady's intercession that formed this apostolate. Angel members must always follow Her example of humility.

We can help each other on Earth out of love. In Heaven, love is perfected, and souls can help us on Earth even more. The communion of saints will be a great aid to Angel members. Members are recommended to read the lives of the saints.

All the saints will help. However, fifteen saints in Heaven will be the patrons of this lay apostolate.

1. Saint Michael the Archangel - Revelation 12 shows that he will help protect us from evil spirits. Pray the Saint Michael Prayer often (Sec. 2.2).

 2. **Saint Gabriel the Archangel -** As he was sent by God to deliver the most important message to a human being, he will help Angel members deliver messages, or evangelize individually and through the mass media.

3. **Saint Raphael the Archangel**
He will protect Angel members on their journeys, help out with healing ministries, encourage works of mercy, and help bring good things into our lives.

4. **Saint Ignatius of Loyola** - He was the founder of the Society of Jesus (Jesuits) who wrote the Spiritual Exercises and will help teach us how to meditate.

5. **Saint Francis Xavier** - He was a Jesuit who learned how to meditate from Saint Ignatius of Loyola and then travelled around the world to teach others how to meditate. He is the patron of missions. He will help us to teach others how to meditate.

6. **Saint Dominic -**

He founded the Order of Preachers and received the Rosary from Our Lady. Countless miracles and conversions occurred with Saint Dominic and his companions. He set up a Democratic Republic form of government for his order that is complete with balance of powers. The USA used St. Dominic's model to set up their government. He will inspire us to pray the Rosary, use it as a weapon, evangelize with it and be humble when miracles occur.

7. **Saint Francis of Assisi**

He founded the Franciscan order, saw Jesus as King of the Angels when he received the stigmata (miraculous wounds of Christ). He also rebuilt a church called Saint Mary of the Angels. He promoted mental prayer by using live animals in the manger scene. He will help Angel members understand Jesus is King by showering graces of humility and simplicity upon us.

8. Saint John the Evangelist

In Revelation 2 and 3, Jesus told him to write a letter to the Angels during the Last Days. He meditated at the foot of the Cross when Jesus was crucified. Jesus said, "There is **no greater love** than this; that a man lay down his life for his friends" (John 15:13). As his Gospel, three letters, and the book of Revelation show, this meditation helped him to understand love more than all the other Scripture writers. He will help Angel members to understand the Cross and true love. St. John is known as an eagle because his soul knew how to fly to Heaven.

9. Saint Mary Magdalen

Meditated at the foot of the Cross when Jesus was crucified. She had complete trust in the infinite mercy of God. She did not despair in the miserable state of slavery she was in but gave glory to God by allowing Him to save her. She listened to the Angel on Easter Sunday and evangelized the Good News to the evangelist. She will help Angel members meditate on the passion, encourage hope for repentant sinners, listen to Angels and rejoice when sinners are converted.

10. **Saint Sr. Faustina** - Jesus appeared to her throughout her life and gave a message of Divine Mercy. She saw an Angel who could not pour out a vial of plagues upon the earth (as described in the Book or Revelation) because people were praying the Chaplet of Divine Mercy. She will help Angel members, ask for mercy, live mercy, evangelize mercy, and have complete trust in Jesus.

11. **Saint Louis DeMontfort**

He was a third order Dominican (O.P.) who wrote *True Devotion to the Blessed Virgin Mary* under guidance of the Holy Spirit. The easiest, surest, fastest, and safest way to become a saint is by being a holy slave of love to Jesus through the Blessed Virgin Mary. Great saints who practice this devotion were predicted to rise up in the Last Days. Saint John Paul II and Blessed Mother Theresa of Calcutta are among them.

If you try to be a saint, or an imitation of Christ by your own efforts, it is like carving a statue out of wood. It is very painful, time consuming, and easy to make big mistakes. An easy, short, surer, and more perfect way is to use a mold. The Blessed Virgin Mary is the perfect mold who God used to form His Son, Jesus. True Devotion is when the Blessed Virgin Mary, our Queen, molds us. Saint Louis DeMontfort will help us to understand True Devotion so that we can become great saints.

12. **Saint Theresa of the Little Flower - Lisieux**
Her vocation was to love. She performed small tasks with great love, which made her a great saint. She wrote the book *Story of a Soul*, which described her little way of love. She is a doctor of the Church and the patroness of missions. She will help Angel members perform their mission with great love and humility.

13.   **St. Joseph of Cupertino** "The Flying Saint" When he meditated, his body flew with his soul. He is also the patron saint of students and will help us learn to meditate.

14. **Saint John Paul II the Great** When darkness was covering the Earth and all seemed lost, he consecrated his pontificate "Totus Tuus " (Totally Yours to Jesus through Mary). The Light shined in the world and the renewal began. Look at his life and ask for his intercession to be a good Angel member.

15. **The Wise Men** They saw the beautiful star and rejoiced greatly. They recognized the sign of the times, went on a pilgrimage, found the Child with Mary, His mother, and, falling down, worshiped Him (see Matthew 2:11). Think of how many excuses they had for not acting. They will help us to act wisely and courageously. In their wisdom, they saw God as a poor, humble, simple, helpless, yet all powerful baby. They will help us to see God as the poor,
humble, simple, helpless, yet all-powerful Eucharist.

ORDER INFORMATION

Help us evangelize Our Lady's message to the spiritually hungry souls.

Angels of the New Era -

The Angels will help you to learn how to meditate so you can direct your pilgrimage on Earth to reach heaven.

Or **The Weapon of Medjugorje** A true story of an engineer who challenged Our Lady of Medjugorje and discovered the true weapon.

5^{00} Add $3.^{00}$ S & H (shipping & handling)

5 for 20^{00} Add $6.^{00}$ S & H

10 for 35^{00} Add $8.^{00}$ S & H

Case of 50 for 150^{00} Add $10.^{00}$ S & H

Our Lady of the Cross

Messages given to Joe Reinholtz at Queen of Heaven Cemetery, Hillside IL.

3^{00} Add $3.00 S & H

10 for $25.^{00}$ Add $6.00 S & H

Case of 50 for $100.^{00}$ Add $10.00 S & H

Also 6" x 9" Evangelization Books.

Journey w Jesus (6"x 9")

Part #1 Blue Book - Review our origins and the Old Testament to prepare us before encountering God in the Holy land.

Part #2 Red Book - Jesus was baptized and then went on to the Galilee area evangelizing.

Part #3 Gold Book - Jesus' mission reaches the culmination in Jerusalem.

Learn all about Jesus Christ as we take you to the Holy Land!

Retreat into the Heart of Mercy (6"x 9") – by Guy Murphy

Plunge into the Divine Heart of Jesus and His Great Mercy.

Unity and Victory St. Maximillian Kolbe – Pope Francis – and President Trump (6"x 9") – by Guy Murphy

Your choice, Prices of the (6"x 9") Books are:

$7.99 each. Add $3.00 (shipping & handling)

5 for $30   Add $6 S & H

Case of 50 for $250.   Add $10 S & H

****

Make checks payable to: Totally Yours Co.
                        P.O. Box 897
                        Hillside, IL 60162

RELATED WEB SITES   www.MEDJ1.com